WALLS that Wow

WALLS that Wow

75 Ideas for Exciting
Room Makeovers

Country Sampler
BOOKS

Country Sampler Books is an imprint of Emmis Books.

For further information, contact the publisher at

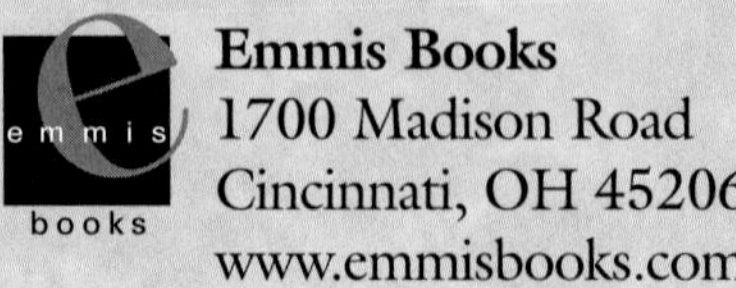

Emmis Books
1700 Madison Road
Cincinnati, OH 45206
www.emmisbooks.com

Library of Congress Cataloging-in-Publication Data

Walls that wow / by the editors of Country Sampler.
p. cm.
Includes index.
ISBN-13: 978-1-57860-224-7
ISBN-10: 1-57860-224-6
1. House painting. 2. Interior walls--decoration. 3. Mural painting and decoration. I. Country Sampler (St. Charles, Ill.)
TT323.W312 2005
698'.142--dc22

2005009788

Edited by Lisa Sloan

Designed by Catherine LePenske

Introduction

Walls set the stage for any room's design. Within these pages, you'll find more than 75 innovative techniques for backgrounds perfectly suited to your personal style be it colorfully dramatic or serenely understated. We've compiled our readers' favorite treatments from past issues of *Country Sampler Decorating Ideas* magazine, and show you how to recreate them at home. Step-by-step instructions make it easy to fashion finishes ranging from old-world plaster and country crackles to tone-on-tone stripes and barely there textures. You'll find all you need (except paint and brushes) to create walls that truly wow.

Hope you enjoy the book,

Ann Wilson

Ann Wilson,
Editor of *Country Sampler Decorating Ideas*

CONTENTS

56

98

68

78

108

118

Some Terms to Know

CRACKLE

CRACKLE—A medium applied between a base coat and topcoat that causes the topcoat to shrink and crack, revealing the base color, for an aged look.

DRY BRUSHING—Softly tinting a previously painted surface using a brush with just a small amount of a different-color paint on the tips of the bristles.

GLAZE BASE—A clear medium designed to be tinted by mixing with paint. Used for many faux finishes, it is semitransparent; the more glaze in the mixture, the more translucent the result.

LIMEWASH—A specialty paint that replicates the age-old finish originally made of slaked lime in water. It has a wonderful surface glow and textured appearance.

RAGGING—Creating a softly mottled effect by either applying (ragging on) or removing (ragging off) glaze or paint with a soft cotton rag.

VENETIAN PLASTER—An effect achieved by layering a colored plaster compound over an opaque base coat. After application, it is highly burnished to a smooth, slightly translucent finish.

WASH—Paint that has been thinned either with water or glaze base.

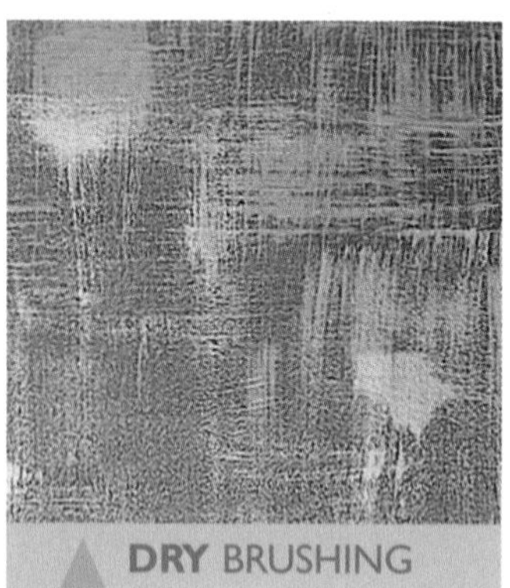

DRY BRUSHING

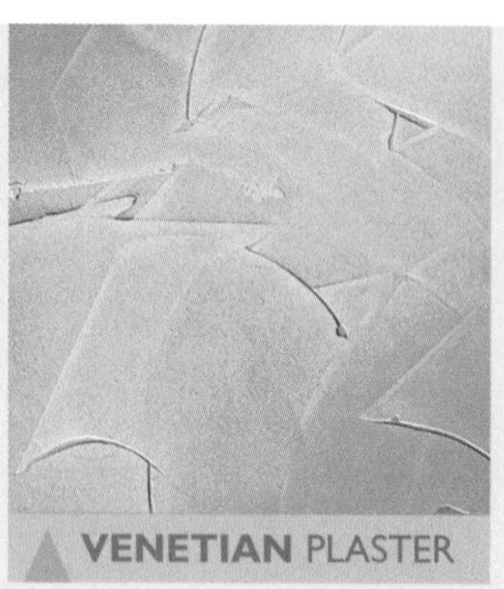

VENETIAN PLASTER

CHOOSING COLOR

■ Color choices are a matter of personal preference, but you can take steps to ensure you pick something you'll love. Take your cue from the furnishings and fabrics in the room. Look at the color wheel to see what colors complement each other, and don't be afraid to seek out advice from your paint dealer. Some paint companies offer online tools that let you "paint" a sample room or even scan in a photo of your own room and colorize it so you can take a hue for a virtual test drive.

TRY BEFORE YOU BUY

■ Try out colors before you buy enough for a whole room. Some manufacturers now sell sample jars containing a few ounces of paint, which can provide you with a better sense of color than a paint chip. You can apply the color either directly to your wall or to a test board. Look at it both during the day and night so you can see how natural and artificial light affect the appearance of the color. If you pick a color and it's not quite right when you get it up on the walls, you may be able to take it back and have it adjusted at the paint shop. For example, your paint dealer may be able to turn a minty green into an apple green with the addition of more yellow pigment.

Tools of the Trade

ARTIST BRUSHES—Small brushes used by artists, these come in many shapes, including flat, round and angled. They are great for adding details and touching up.

CHIP BRUSH—Also called China bristle brush, an inexpensive natural bristle paintbrush used to apply glaze. Its bristles leave brush marks and can be used to create interesting patterns.

SHAPER TOOLS—Rubber- or silicone-tipped tools that come in various shapes, sizes and levels of firmness. They are used to carve images in wet paint or glaze.

FAUX-FINISHING TROWEL—A stainless-steel tool with rounded edges used for plaster and other textured finishes.

JAPAN SCRAPER—A flexible stainless-steel tool that looks like a putty knife with rounded edges. It's used for Venetian plaster and dimensional stenciling.

PAD PAINTER— A square pad attached to a short handle that can be used instead of a roller or to cut in around trim.

PAINTERS TAPE—Specialty low-tack tape available in various widths. It is used to protect areas from paint and mask off patterns, like stripes or borders. Remove tape before paint is completely dry for best results.

ROLLERS— These come in various sizes and textures. Smooth rollers, like foam, are best for smooth surfaces, while longer-nap rollers are best for rougher surfaces. Use a 9" standard-size roller for base coating; try smaller rollers for specialty finishes.

SEA SPONGE—A natural sponge used to create mottled effects. It is preferred by professional painters for its irregular texture, resilience and absorption. (A synthetic sponge is too even and regular for faux effects.)

SOFTENING BRUSH—A wide, soft specialty brush with natural bristles. It is used to soften and blend colored glazes in techniques like colorwashing, graining, ragging and marbling.

STIPPLING BRUSH—A blocky, palm-held brush with long, firm, dense bristles. It is used to create a lightly flecked finish or blend glazes when pounced over a painted surface.

ROCKER-STYLE WOOD-GRAINING TOOL—A tool with a molded rubber surface used to produce a realistic pattern of the heart grain of wood.

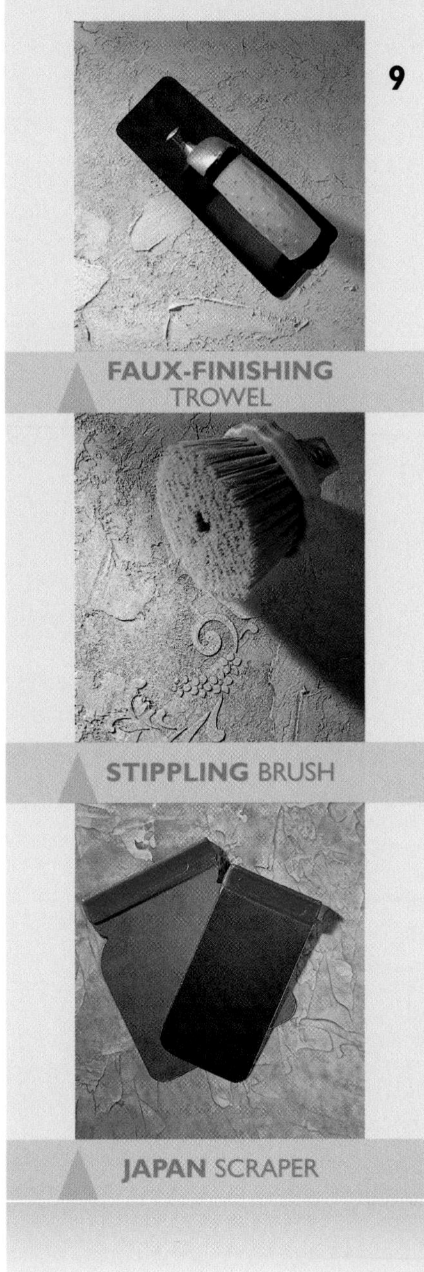

FAUX-FINISHING TROWEL

STIPPLING BRUSH

JAPAN SCRAPER

A NOTE ABOUT PAINT

■ All of our projects are done with latex or water-based paints, such as craft acrylics. While many decorative painters prefer to work with alkyd or oil-based products because they have a longer drying time, which allows more time to manipulate the finish, we recommend latex because it offers easier cleanup and less-pungent fumes. When you need to extend the dry time of latex paint for a project, we recommend adding glaze or a clear paint conditioner.

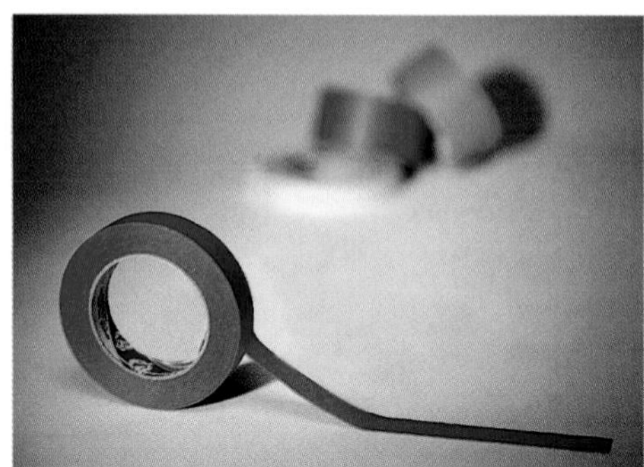

Prepping Walls for Painting

To get the most out of your paint treatment, make sure your walls are properly prepared before beginning.

- Clean walls before starting. Wipe or vacuum away cobwebs and dust. If walls are dirty or greasy, wash with a mild detergent or degreaser. Rinse away all residue and let dry well.
- Scrape away any flaking paint.
- Patch things up. Fill in any small holes using spackling compound. Let dry, sand and wipe with a tack cloth. Use acrylic painters caulk for small cracks. For larger holes, you may need to use patching tape and joint compound.
- Tape off walls, trim, mirrors, etc. with low-tack painters tape. Remove or loosen light fixture covers, outlet covers and switch plates so you can paint behind them. Protect floors and furnishings with drop cloths or long strips of cardboard. (For floors, try to use an absorbent cloth to avoid transferring paint drips to your shoes.)
- Apply a coat of primer, if needed. New, unpainted walls especially need primer to seal the surface and allow paint to adhere properly. Stained areas and patched areas should also be primed. (Check with your paint retailer for the best type for the job; see Special Situations for more information.)
- Before applying any new paper treatment to your wall, apply a coat of sizing to the area. This will ensure easy removal in the future.

SPECIAL SITUATIONS:

PREVIOUSLY PAPERED WALLS—If you have removed wallpaper from the surface, be sure you have also removed all traces of glue from the wall with a thorough washing. Any leftover paste will react with the water in latex products. To ensure a smooth surface, you may want to prep the wall with an oil-based stain-blocking primer.

DARK-COLORED WALLS—If you are making a big change or using a deep, dark color for your new finish, consider having your primer tinted to match the paint color. This cuts down on the number of coats you'll need to cover the surface.

GLOSSY FINISH—Sand wall before painting to dull the surface.

WALLS IN BAD SHAPE—Use a treatment that takes advantage of this, such as something with an aged look, or you can apply a lightweight lining paper to the walls first and then paint over that.

TIP: *If you have to pause during your project, you can keep your paintbrush workable by wrapping it in plastic wrap or foil. If you're working with a roller, use a plastic clamshell-like tray that closes.*

BASE-COATING BASICS

■ Begin by "cutting in"—use a paintbrush or paint pad to paint the edges around a window or door frame and where the walls and ceiling meet.

■ Next, paint the ceiling, using a roller extension pole to expand your reach. Painting the ceiling first ensures you won't drip or splatter ceiling paint on the walls.

■ Choose the right roller for your wall texture (see page 9).

■ Randomly run the roller up and down the wall and from side to side in a zigzag pattern, working in an approximate 3-foot-square area. Spread the paint evenly and try not to slide the roller across the wall. To complete an area, lift off in an upward stroke. When you move to the next area, blend by rolling over the wet edges.

PRACTICE MAKES PERFECT

BEFORE YOU SET to work on your walls, practice all techniques on a test board. This not only ensures you are comfortable applying the finish and working with the tools, but also provides an opportunity to try out and adjust paint-to-glaze ratios. It also allows you to check color combinations—you can temporarily tape the finished board to the wall for a preview. Make the board from a piece of foamboard. Prepare the board in the same manner as you would prepare the wall, applying any necessary primer, etc. You could also try out the technique in a hidden area of the room first, such as in a closet or behind a door.

SAFETY FIRST

PLEASE READ all manufacturer's instructions for proper usage of the product before beginning. Work in a well-ventilated area and wear a dust mask and/or goggles, if needed. Because paints and some cleaning solvents can irritate the skin, wear protective gloves. If you'll be painting the ceiling or working on the upper walls, be sure to stand on a steady, level base.

CLEANUP

TO GET THE MAXIMUM use from your brushes, be sure to clean them properly after every project, following the paint manufacturer's instructions. Latex paint can usually be washed off in warm running water. Use a flat-bladed knife to scrape off most of the paint before rinsing. As you rinse, gently separate the bristles and be sure to work on the base of the brush. You may need to add some mild detergent, but be sure to thoroughly rinse. When the brush is clean, give it a few good shakes to fluff up the bristles. Clean rollers and pads the same way, but roll excess paint onto newspaper before rinsing.

WASHED *in Color*

14

LOOKING FOR A VERSATILE and easy paint treatment that suits both rustic and contemporary interiors? Give colorwashing a try. This technique involves applying one or more thin, transparent colored glazes over a base color. The random application produces a soft, dappled surface, while visible brush-strokes and drips add an element of texture. Your color choices determine the effect. For example, golden hues speak of sunlight while blues suggest rippling water. Use colorwashing alone to lend depth and drama to your walls, or combine it with other effects, like stenciling or stamping, for added interest.

TIP: *This technique works best with two people—one person to apply the paint with a roller and another to make long, horizontal brush strokes in the rolled-on paint. The first person can then come back with the stippling brush to further blend the paint colors as they change value. This team effort ensures that you can manipulate the paint before it dries and allows for a more uniform look.*

DAWNING *Color*

1. Base-coat wall with light lavender paint. Let dry.

2. Using a yardstick level, measure up 2 feet from the baseboard with a colored pencil, and draw a straight horizontal guideline across the wall. (Use a colored pencil lighter than the color that will be painted in that area.) Measure and mark a second horizontal guideline on the wall 4 feet from the baseboard (see photo A).

3. Create glaze mixtures using the three remaining paint colors. Mix each in a separate lined paint tray, using a ratio of one part paint to three parts glaze.

4. With a foam roller, horizontally apply the darkest glaze mixture (deep violet) to the wall, starting at the baseboard and extending about 6 inches above the first marked guideline (see photo B).

5. Add texture by using a 3" paintbrush to brush long, horizontal strokes across the wall in the rolled-on paint (see photo C).

6. With the same foam roller, apply the midtone glaze mixture (medium purple), beginning at the first 2-foot marked guideline and continuing about 6 inches above the 4-foot marked guideline. The 6-inch area above the guideline will be blended when you apply the next layer. (Once you begin painting with the lighter color, do not paint below the previous guideline; the dark and mid-tone colors should only overlap in the 6-inch areas above the guidelines.)

7. Using the paintbrush, repeat the process as above, creating long, horizontal strokes in the rolled-on paint. Continue blending up the wall, but do not blend the second paint color above the marked 4-foot guideline.

8. Use the same roller to apply the lightest glaze mixture (lilac). Overlap the midtone color, beginning at the 4-foot guideline, and continue to the ceiling. Repeat the same horizontal brush strokes after rolling on the paint.

8. Blend the wall colors with a stippling brush. Begin at the baseboard and pounce the stippling brush horizontally across the wall to soften the paint colors together wherever they meet (see photo D). Wipe off excess paint/glaze on a rag when needed. Vary the direction of the brush with your wrist, gradually moving up the wall as you work. Avoid going back over completed areas, as you risk introducing the wrong color into a section.

SHOPPING LIST

- Flat latex paint in light lavender, lilac, medium purple and deep violet (all hues from one paint strip—see box)
- Yardstick level
- Lilac colored pencil
- 4 paint trays with liners
- Glaze base
- Foam roller
- 3" paintbrush
- Stippling brush
- Rag

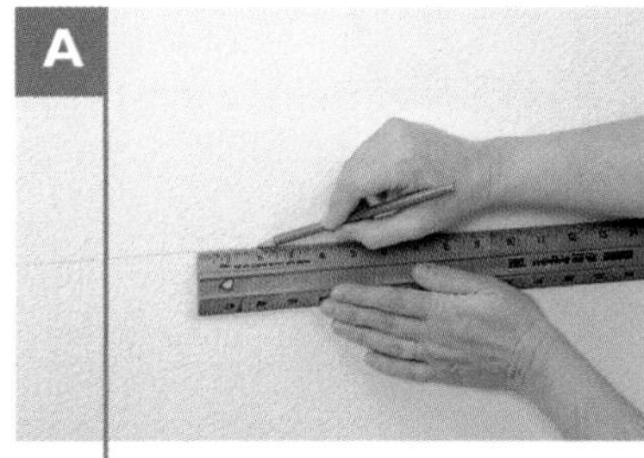
A

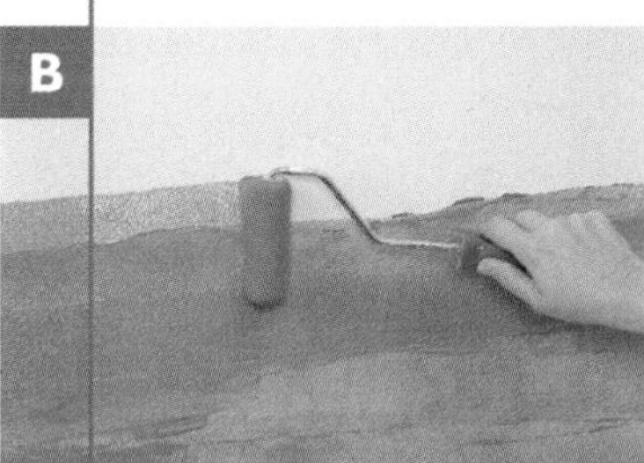
B

C

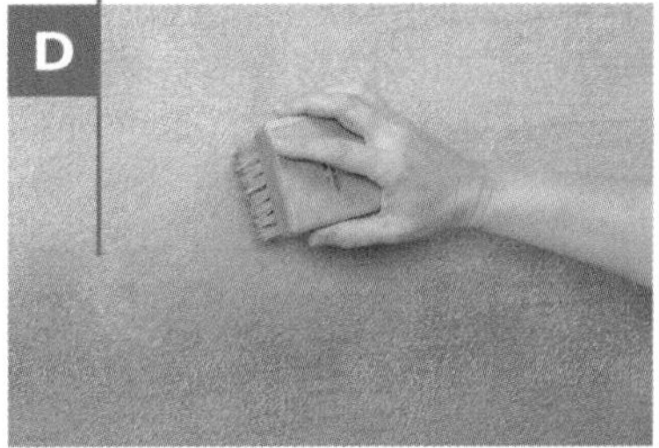
D

PLUCKED FROM A PAINT STRIP

TAKING ITS CUE FROM NATURE, this treatment blends different values of the same color, graduating from dark to light, to produce a subtle effect, like the night sky fading into the lavender light of early morning. Though we used shades of purple, you can use any color, working from the set of shades on a single seven-hue paint strip. For the base coat, use the second lightest shade, then select the fourth, fifth and sixth colors on the strip, blending them with glaze to create the gradient treatment. You might try yellows for a sunlit effect or deepening blues to reflect the night sky. Or combine the two, so the two phases of the sky start at opposing sides of the room or wall and blend together as you work to the middle.

WATERCOLOR *Wash*

1. You will be applying washes to the wall by alternating ragging and brushing techniques. Larger areas will be ragged; smaller patches in between will be brushed and blended into the ragged area.

2. Base-coat ceiling with dusty rose paint. Let dry. Base-coat walls with sunshine yellow paint. Let dry.

3. Create a wash by mixing a ratio of one part deep rose paint to one part water. Do the same with the deep coral paint. Mix well.

4. Plan to randomly apply the ragged-on wash in irregular 3-foot patches around the entire room, leaving spaces between the patches to fill with the brushing technique.

5. Place a rag into each container. Wearing rubber gloves, wring most of the paint from rags. Bunch up a rag in each hand. Pat the rags onto the wall, alternating the two colorwashes (see photo A). To create faint watercolor-like impressions, work outward until the rags run out of color. If the color is too strong in some spots, blend with a lighter wash or lift off color with a clean, damp rag.

6. Dip a 4" paintbrush in the deep coral wash and apply to the wall randomly in approximately 1-foot by 1-foot sections. Use the rags from the previous step to quickly pull off most of the paint, leaving some drips and runs (see photo B). As you work, step back from the wall to determine whether you need to add or remove color in any areas. Let dry.

7. If desired, highlight corners and areas around doorways with softly colored flowers, stems and leaves, using acrylic paints (see box). Place the designs so they seem to twine up the wall and onto the ceiling or appear as if they're growing out of door and window trim.

SHOPPING LIST

- Flat latex paint in dusty rose, sunshine yellow, deep rose and deep coral
- Water
- 2 large containers with lids
- Rags
- Rubber gloves
- 4" paintbrush
- Round artist brush
- Acrylic craft paints in wine, rose, leaf green and light green

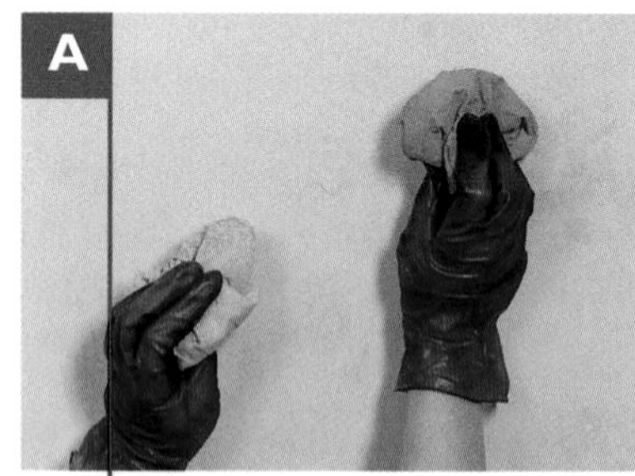
A

B

HANDPAINTED FLORALS

TO EASILY EMBELLISH YOUR WATERCOLOR WALLS, add soft floral touches in random spots. Copy and enlarge flower patterns (pulled from fabric, art or another source) to a size that suits your walls. With transfer paper and a pencil, copy the shapes onto the wall in desired locations. Use both latex and acrylic paints to paint the leaf and floral details, blending new colors to suit your palette, if needed. Thin each paint color, using a ratio of one part water to one part paint. Paint stems and leaves first, using a liner brush to apply the outlines, followed by a clean, wet round brush to pull the paint from the outline into the center. Paint the flowers in the same manner.

STONE Age

1. Base-coat walls with off-white paint. Let dry. Tape off ceiling.

2. Mix 5 cups of water with 1 tablespoon of charcoal paint in a plastic container to create a wash. Wear latex gloves. Dip a sea sponge in gray wash; squeeze excess wash from sponge.

3. Beginning at the top of the wall and working downward in 3-foot sections, sponge the charcoal wash randomly on the wall, allowing some of the base coat to show through (see photo A). Let a few drips run; these imperfections add weathered charm. Application of wash should be light for a subtle effect. Let dry.

4. Mix 5 cups of water with 1 tablespoon of medium gold paint in a plastic container. Apply mixture randomly with sea sponge as above, allowing some of the charcoal wash to show through (see photo B). Let dry.

5. Pour a small amount of charcoal paint on a foam plate. Very lightly dry brush vertical sections on the wall to create texture. To begin, dip the tips of a 2" brush into paint, and wipe off excess on a paper towel. Apply paint using a vertical motion, creating streaks of different lengths and thicknesses. Leave heavier paint streaks in some areas (see photo C). Let dry.

6. Dry brush off-white paint over charcoal streaks. Let dry.

7. Apply charcoal paint to scripted stamp with a foam brush. (Rubber stamps are available with a variety of scripted sayings, from well-known quotations to free-flowing text. We chose a rectangular-shaped block of French text.) Stamp the scripted sayings on select areas of the wall (see photo D). Let dry.

ORIGINS OF COLORWASHING

IN OLD FRENCH HOMES, the plaster walls were painted with distemper—a mix of glue, water, chalk and pigment. The surface required repainting every few years, but before doing so, the painters would wash off the water-soluble distemper. Faint streaks of the color (and sometimes previously applied colors) were left behind, and this residue became part of the new painted finish. Today, we get a similar look by applying several "washes" (paint thinned with glaze or water), leaving brush strokes and drips for an authentic look. Here, the streaks and drips of darker washes against a light background combine with dry brushing and stamping to suggest a façade eroded by natural elements.

SHOPPING LIST

- Flat latex paint in off-white, charcoal and medium gold
- Painters tape
- Water
- Plastic containers
- Latex gloves
- Sea sponges
- Foam plates
- Paper towels
- Two 2" flat paintbrushes
- Small foam brush
- Rubber stamp with script design

A

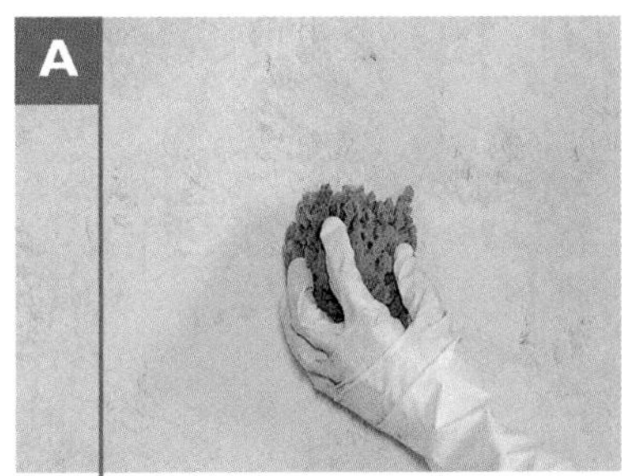

B

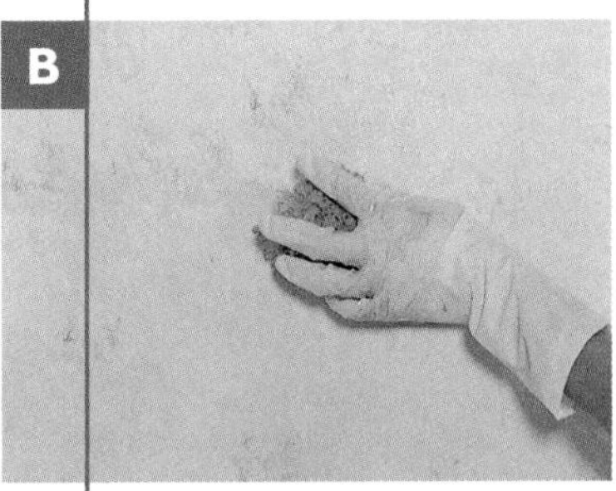

C

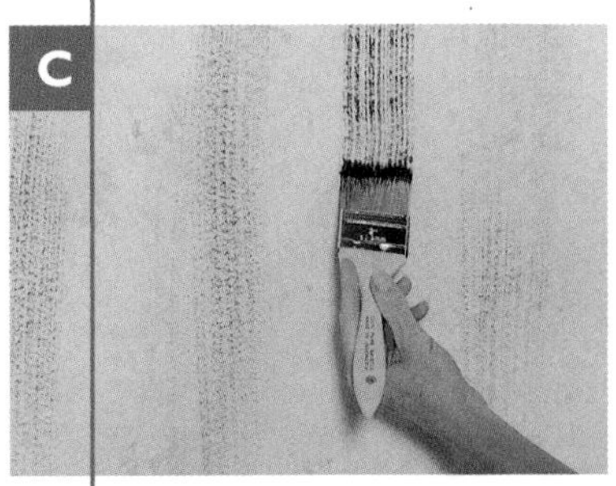

D

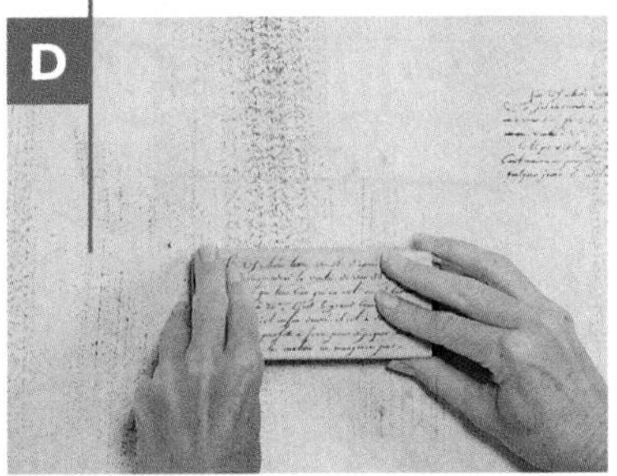

LUSHLY *Layered*

1. Base-coat wall with medium olive green paint.

2. Mix glaze with medium yellow-green paint in a plastic container, using two parts paint to one part glaze. Set aside.

3. Pour straight glaze base in one corner of the paint tray. In the opposite corner, pour dark yellow green paint. Because the paint and glaze are of similar consistency, the two liquids should fill both halves of the tray but not blend together. This allows you to simultaneously load your roller with equal amounts of glaze and paint (see photo A). Lightly roll a 9" foam roller into the top of the mix. Do not push the roller in too deeply or the paint and glaze may overflow and blend together. (When you reload the roller, place it into the tray in the same direction to avoid accidentally blending the paint and glaze.)

4. Roll the glaze and paint combination onto the wall, working in irregularly shaped 4-foot by 4-foot sections. Allow large portions of the base coat to show through. As you work, the paint will blend with the glaze on the wall, producing a dappled effect with some spots having more paint than others. Continue to move across the wall, blending each new section with the previous one.

5. Pour mixed medium yellow-green glaze into a fresh paint tray. While the first glaze coat is still wet, use 4" roller to randomly apply medium yellow-green to selected areas, blending over the darker glaze and filling in some areas where the base coat is visible.

6. In some areas, use a rag and/or a chip brush to apply, blend and blot the two glaze colors together for a subtle, translucent effect (see photo B).

7. As you work, step back often and examine the treatment from a distance. Look for spots containing too much of the same color or a heavier application of paint. Blend these areas into the rest of the treatment by adding more light or dark glaze with a small roller or brush. Apply more base-coat color if needed.

8. To soften areas, apply a glaze, then wipe down the surface with a rag. Let glaze sit for a few minutes until it starts to set up, then pat or wipe off, leaving some of the color on the surface and blending it into surrounding areas.

9. To cover harsh roller lines or blotches, use straight paint, dry brushed in irregular-shaped patches on wall. Pick up any of the three paint colors with the tips of a dry chip brush and sweep the brush back and forth over the area, carefully blending edges (see photo C).

SHOPPING LIST

- Flat latex paint in medium olive green, medium yellow-green and dark yellow-green
- Glaze base
- Large plastic container with lid
- Paint trays and liners
- 9" foam roller
- 4" woven cotton roller
- Rags
- 3" chip paintbrushes

A

B

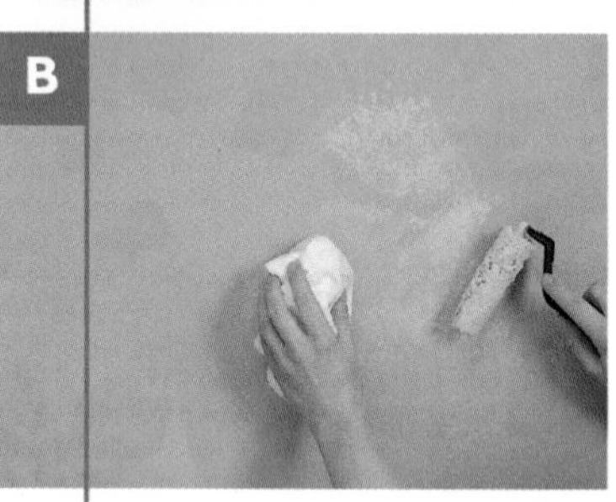

C

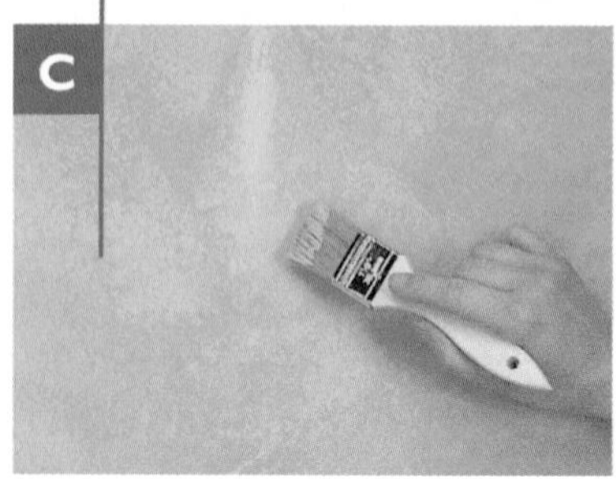

RUBBED GLAZES

THIS TREATMENT OWES ITS VARIEGATED appearance not only to the pair of paint washes, but to the different tools used—rollers, brushes and rags. Rags are used to rub off some of the glaze to blend and soften the look of the treatment. For a simpler variegated surface, you can also use rags to create a rubbed-on effect. Working in small irregular sections, rub a deeper glaze over a lighter base color, using small, circular movements. Continue moving outward until the glaze fades into the wall, blending sections together as you work. The result will be a lightly swirled surface with enough variation to hide wall imperfections.

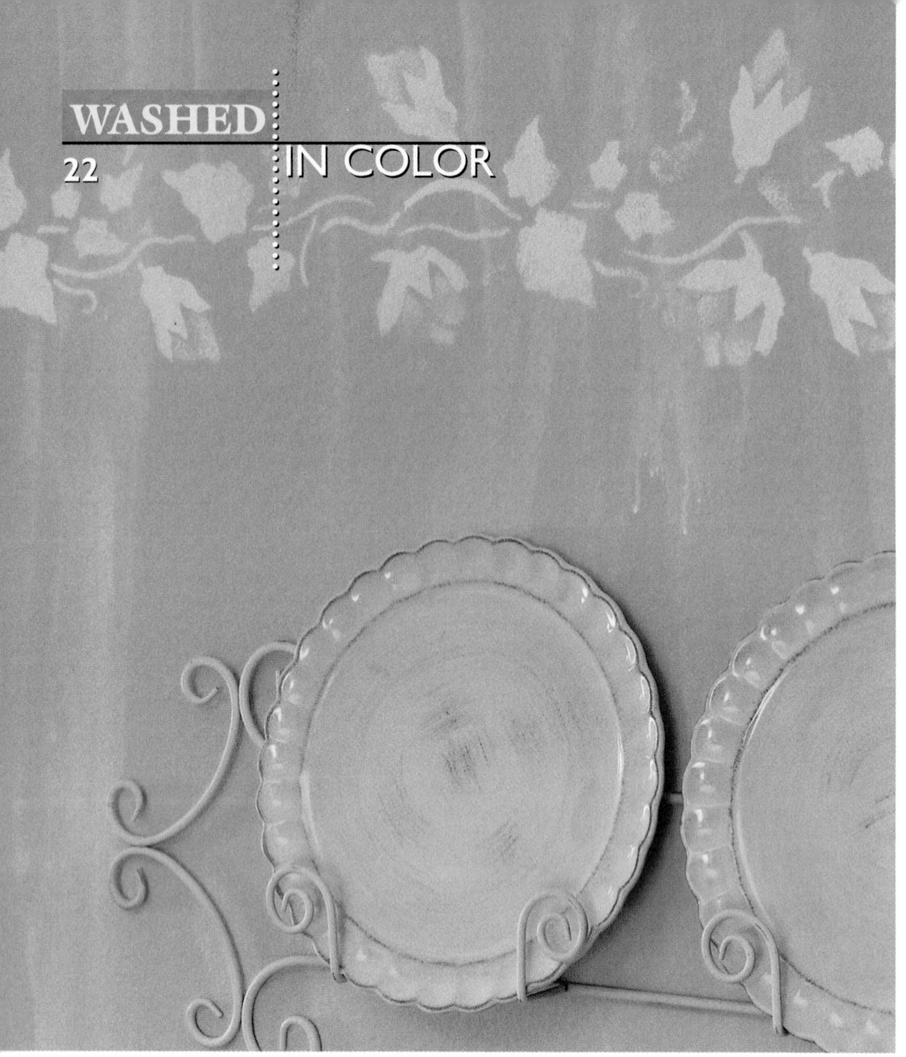

SOFTLY *Streaked*

THESE WALLS ARE WASHED WITH BLUE and given dimension and a vaguely striped effect by streaks of cream and brown wash. Base-coat the walls with sky blue paint. Let dry. Start at the midpoint on your wall and work out toward the corners. Every 3 feet or so, use a pencil and yardstick level to lightly mark a few vertical guidelines on the wall. In a plastic container, mix one part cream paint with one part water. In another plastic container, mix a small amount of brown acrylic paint with six parts water. (Be sure to test washes on a board. If cream streaks are too opaque, add more water; if they are too transparent, add a bit more paint. Brown pigment can be very strong, so a little paint goes a long way. If the brown wash is too dark, add more water or a small amount of cream wash.) Dip a paint pad into the cream wash and apply long, smooth vertical strokes, randomly spacing them roughly 1 foot apart. The streaks should feather out at top and bottom. Let the paint drip and run occasionally, patting with a rag for texture. Vary spacing between strokes. Reach as far up and down as you can; you can go back later and extend the streaks by blending in new strokes to the ceiling or floor. Blend carefully and vary stopping and starting points to avoid creating the appearance of a horizontal pattern that will detract from the look of the treatment. Repeat the process with the brown wash, applying the brown streaks more randomly and spaced further apart than the cream streaks. Again, carefully blend streaks up to the ceiling and down to the floor. Erase any pencil marks.

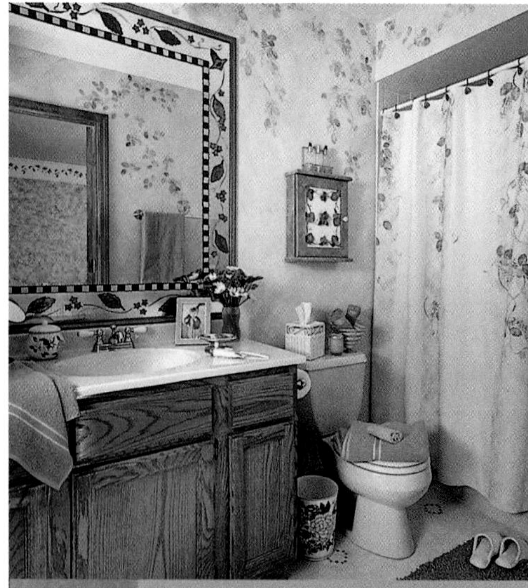

OLD COUNTRY

ACHIEVE THE CAREWORN LOOK of a Tuscan villa twined with vines by colorwashing over floral stamps. Purchase flower and leaf stamps or blocks. Begin by base-coating your walls with warm white paint. Let dry. In separate containers, mix two shades of green paint with glaze, using about one part paint to one part glaze. Apply leaf stamps randomly to the wall, varying the direction of the stamp and the color used. Stamp some leaves in bunches; others alone. Mix two shades of purple paint with glaze as above, creating one dark purple and one light purple mixture. Stamp clusters of blooms using both purple glazes. Let dry. With an angled artist brush, paint vines connecting the flowers in both shades of green. Let dry. Mix one part taupe paint, one part glaze and two parts water to make the wash. Dip a stiff-bristled paintbrush into the wash and dab excess on a paper towel. Apply the wash with crosshatched strokes, starting in the corners and working across the wall. The more you brush the surface, the softer the look. To further soften and blend, brush over the damp surface with a soft, natural-bristled brush.

BLUE SKIES

A COOL BLUE WASH refreshes tired walls and recalls wispy clouds drifting across the summer sky. Base-coat your walls with white semi-gloss paint using random strokes with a foam roller. (For a more textured look, use a 3" paintbrush). Let dry. Mix seven parts glaze with two parts sky blue paint and one part water to make the wash. Working in random 1-foot sections, apply the wash with a 3" brush using random strokes. While the glaze is still wet, go over the area using a stiff-bristled brush to make quick, random strokes. This thins out the initial layer of wash and picks up excess paint while adding pattern. Before the wash dries completely, skim the surface of the painted area with a natural-bristle blending brush, flicking the edges of the bristles over the glaze to soften brush strokes and create a cloudy appearance. Move to the next 1-foot section and apply paint as above, using the blending brush to soften the edges between each section. Continue until the wall is complete.

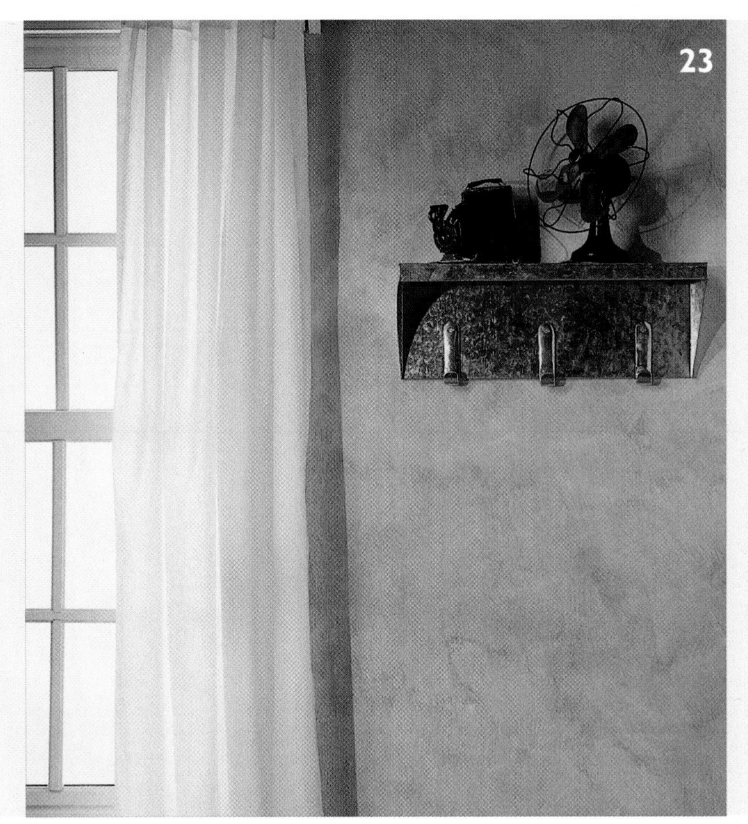

TERRA-COTTA *Treasure*

TWO SHADES OF TERRA-COTTA glaze and oak stain bathe walls in warmth; a once-over with a scrub brush and drips of whitewash add dimension and variation to the finish. Base-coat walls with off-white paint. Let dry. In separate buckets, mix two shades of terra-cotta satin-finish latex paint with clear glaze, using one part paint to one part glaze. Apply the two glazes to the wall with a brush, making short arched strokes. Alternate colors as you work across the wall, allowing the base coat to show through in some areas. Let dry. Using a clean, damp brush, quickly dip bristles into the oak stain and scrub along the wall in a vertical direction to highlight certain areas with a darker color. Let the stain dry for 2 to 4 hours. For a mottled surface, scrub the walls with a damp, stiff-bristled scrub brush, working from the top down in 2- to 3-foot sections. Thin white paint with water, using one part paint to one part water. Dip brush into thinned paint and hold against the top of the wall, allowing paint to drip down. Vary coverage across the wall. When drips have stopped moving, gently blot with a clean dry rag, taking care not to disturb the pattern. Continue working around the room until the treatment is complete.

FAUX *Real*

WORK A LITTLE PAINT MAGIC and create the illusion that your ordinary drywall is covered with burnished driftwood, vintage wallpaper, layered plaster, stone and more. Specialty tools and paints make it easy to produce amazing effects that will have friends guessing whether your walls are authentic or pure artistry. Use the techniques for an entire room or an area you wish to highlight. Either way, the results are sure to be one-of-a-kind.

MARK EMMERSON
MARK EMM

DRIFTWOOD *Finishes*

1. Base-coat wall with pewter gray paint. Let dry. Apply a second coat, if needed. Let dry.

2. Dip a chip brush into the limewash and blot it onto a paper towel to remove excess glaze. Use the 2" brush near the ceiling and in the corners and the 3" brush everywhere else. Beginning near the ceiling, drag the limewash down the wall (see photo A). (Always drag straight down; occasionally hold the brush vertically to form a narrower streak and vary the look.)

3. Before applying limewash to another section, wad a 3-foot piece of dampened cheesecloth into a loose ball and gently drag it over the wet limewash in some areas. This will produce a weathered look. As you work from one section to another, slightly overlap newly applied limewash onto finished areas to blend.

4. Apply a thicker coat of limewash where you want a wood-grain look. Then, drag and rock the wood-graining tool slowly through the wet limewash to create the grain (see photo B). (Don't try to make long strips of wood grain extending from floor to ceiling—stick to strokes between 3 feet and 4 feet long, about the size of short boards.)

5. While the paint is still wet, softly drag the 3" chip brush over the wood-grained area to blend and soften any harsh edges.

SHOPPING LIST

- Pearl-finish latex paint in pewter gray and white
- Textured limewash finish
- 2" and 3" chip brushes
- Rocker-style wood-graining tool
- Cheesecloth
- Paper towels

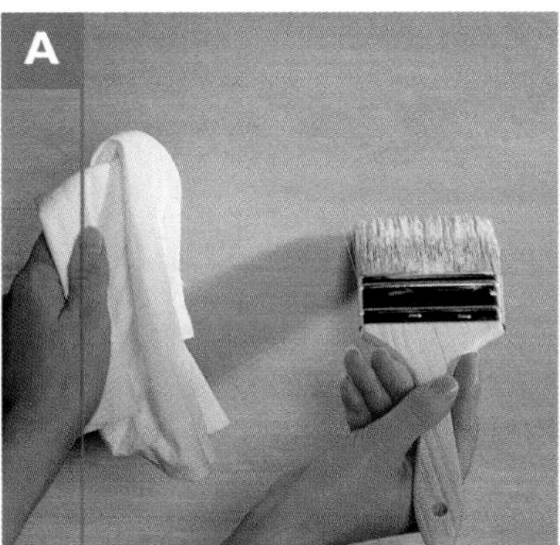

A

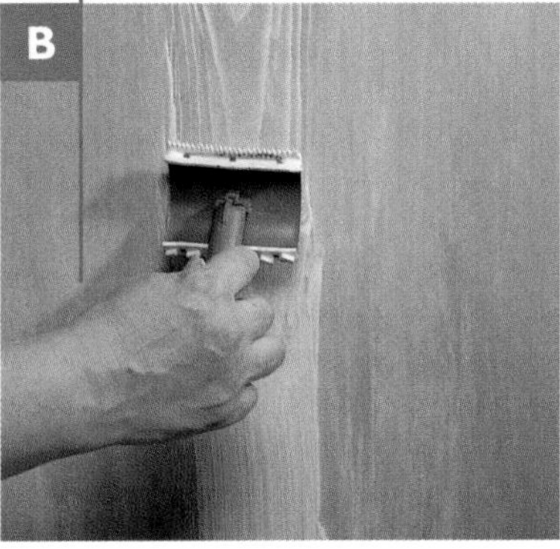

B

GRAINING TIPS

TO CREATE THE SEA-CARESSED SMOOTHNESS of driftwood, use the wood-graining tool sparingly, adding just a hint of dimensional grain to random areas on the wall. This simulates grain without overdoing it.

- Use this finish on nearly any flat surface, but avoid carved areas or moldings. It works well in most settings, from country to modern, and you can use any color. If you want the finished treatment to look like real wood, make sure your color choices are appropriate, like the soft gray we used here.
- As you work, if you're unhappy with the effect, brush over the wet area, apply more limewash, if needed, and begin again. For big mistakes, let dry completely, apply base color and start over from scratch.

FADED *Beauty*

1. Base-coat the wall with cinnamon paint. Let dry.

2. Mix one part mauve paint with two parts water or glaze in a container with a lid. Do the same for wine paint.

3. Apply the mauve glaze mixture to the wall with a brush and blend with a rag until you achieve a soft, lightly distressed look as a background for your stencil design (see photo A). Vary the application so that some areas are lighter and others are heavier. Continue in this manner, working on random areas of the wall, leaving some areas open for adding darker glaze. Let dry. (Adding patches of rubbed glaze gives the treatment dimension.)

4. Repeat the same technique with wine glaze mixture to create a soft, darker, aged look in random areas of the wall. Allow patches of base coat to show in some areas. Let paint dry.

5. Determine stencil placement on the wall and how and where the repeat will occur. Apply stencil adhesive to back of stencil. Place stencil on the wall, making sure that all of the stencil's cutout sections are flat against the wall. Make registration marks with a pencil.

6. With a stencil brush, apply light pink paint to a portion of the stencil (see photo B). Cover only about a quarter to a third of the stencil, allowing some of the base color to show through.

7. Dampen a sea sponge and squeeze out excess water. Dab it into mauve paint and pat off excess on a paper towel. Apply lightly over another third of the stencil, slightly overlapping some of the previously painted section.

8. Dampen a new sea sponge and squeeze out excess water. Dab it into wine paint and pat excess onto a paper towel. Apply lightly over the remaining third of the stencil, overlapping some of the previously painted portions as well (see photo C). (Allow the natural sponge pattern to appear on the stencil. This is what gives it the worn look.)

9. Slowly peel the stencil from the wall, checking to see whether the effect is pleasing. If not, reapply stencil and touch up. Remove stencil from wall.

10. Reposition stencil for the next repeat following the registration marks. If needed, reapply adhesive.

11. Repeat process, this time varying the application of color on the stencil. Each stencil application will be slightly different. The color distribution on the wall should be visually balanced, yet random, to create the illusion of age. Continue stenciling until the wall is complete. Let dry.

SHOPPING LIST

- Flat latex paint in cinnamon, mauve, wine and light pink
- Glaze base or water
- Containers with lids
- 3" paintbrushes
- Rags
- Large-scale scrolled-leaf stencil
- Stencil spray adhesive
- Pencil
- Stencil brush
- Sea sponges
- Paper towels

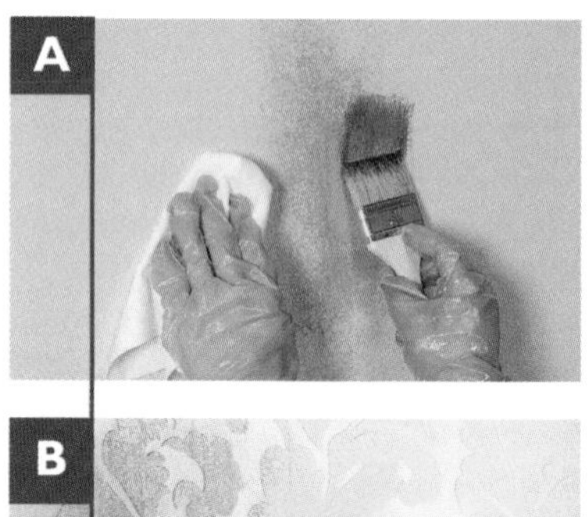
A

B

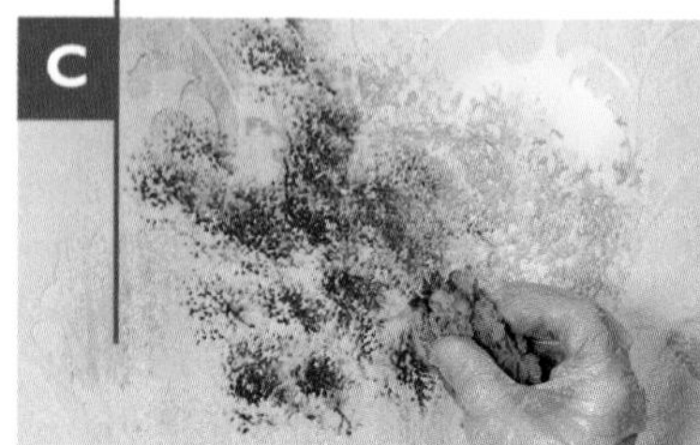
C

SIMPLY UNDERSTATED

FOR A MORE SUBTLE EFFECT, try a tone-on-tone treatment in shades of cream. Use an oversize damask stencil and two shades of cream paint. Base-coat the walls with the darker color, then create two glazes. For the first, mix two parts of the lighter color, one part of the darker color and one part glaze. For the second, mix three parts of the lighter color to one part glaze. Using portions of the large stencil, create an irregular overlapping design across the walls using the darker glaze, then repeat the process with the lighter glaze.

PLASTER *Pretender*

1. Base-coat wall with purple paint. Let dry.

2. Load the surface of the trowel with a thick coating of pink paint using a foam brush. Starting at one of the top corners of the wall, pull the trowel down until the paint no longer transfers to the wall (see photo A). Repeat, working your way to the bottom of the wall in sections. Vary paint coverage from area to area. Let dry. Do not cover all the purple.

3. Apply dark yellow paint using the same technique. Let dry. Make sure to cover some of the purple, but also to overlap the pink (see photo B).

4. Apply the light yellow in same fashion. Let dry. When you are finished, there should be a visual balance of all the colors. Apply more pink or yellow paint, if necessary. Let dry.

5. In a plastic container, mix one part white paint with four parts glaze. Apply mixture to the wall with a roller (see photo C). As you work, use a rag to lightly wipe away some of the white glaze until you have a soft, translucent blend of color. Let dry.

SHOPPING LIST

- Flat latex paint in purple, pink, dark yellow, light yellow and white
- Foam brushes
- 6" plastic trowel
- Glaze base
- Plastic container
- Foam roller
- Rags

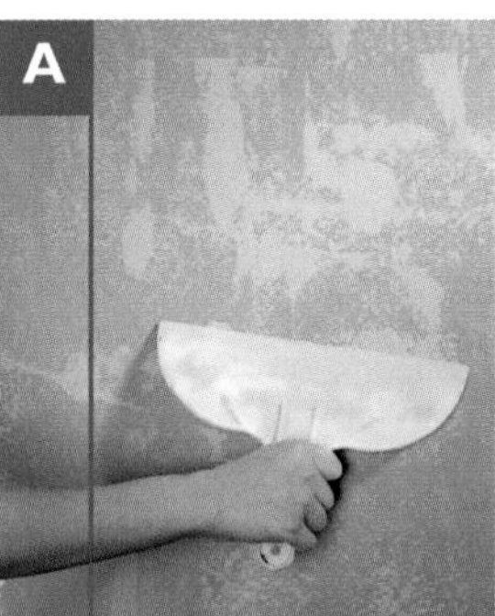
A

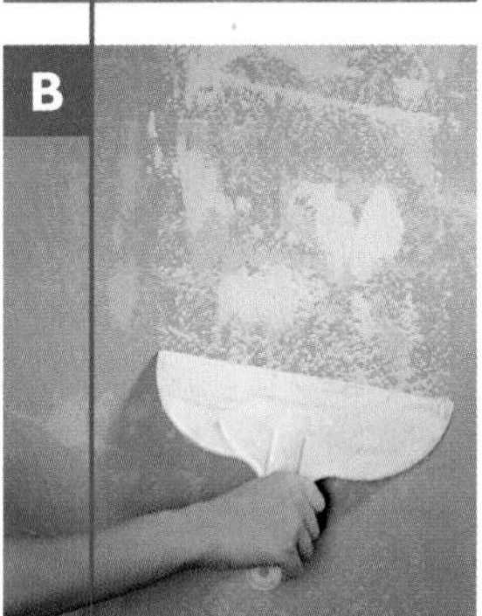
B

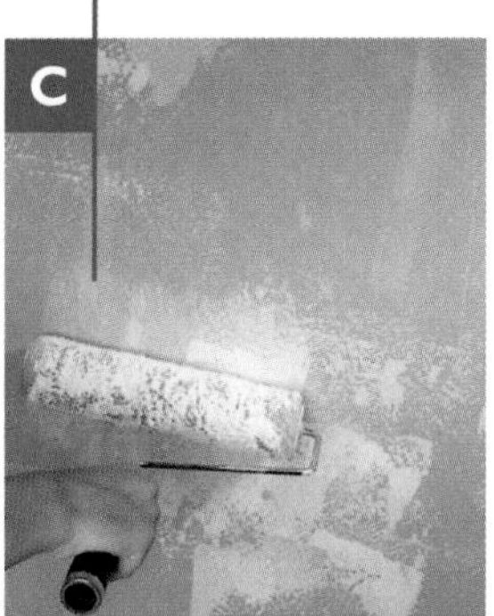
C

THE REAL DEAL

ADD REAL PLASTER TO YOUR WALLS for an even more authentic effect. Base-coat walls with two coats of orange (or another deep, warm color) paint. Let dry. Rub some water-based oak stain onto the walls, using a damp cotton rag to create a dirty, aged appearance. While the wall is drying, plan crack placement on paper, then lightly pencil placement on dry wall. With a clean rag, apply a coat of paste wax inside the marked areas—this will allow you to chip off the Plaster of Paris topcoat later. Prepare Plaster of Paris and a batch of plaster wall patch in separate containers, following manufacturer's instructions, and apply a coat of each to the wall using a plaster float tool. Use broad strokes and alternate types of plaster to create a rough, two-toned effect. Let dry for 24 hours. Referring to your planning sheet and pencil marks, gently tap selected areas on wall with a hammer to crack the plaster. Use a scraper to help pull up plaster layer. Sand the edges of the cracks, then apply clear satin water-based sealer to protect the finish.

TERRY CLOTH *Tiles*

PUT YOUR OLD TERRY CLOTH TOWELS TO GOOD USE—turn them into paint stamps to create a faux-tile wall. Base-coat walls with a light, creamy mustard-colored latex paint. Pick two or three other colors a few shades darker than the base coat to highlight the squares. In separate containers, mix each of the darker colors with glaze base using one part paint to three parts glaze. Wrap terry cloth toweling around a 12-inch square of cardboard, and use duct tape to secure the towel to the back of the cardboard. Make one square for each glaze color. Working with one color at a time, apply glaze mixture to the towel stamp with a short-nap foam roller. Beginning at the bottom of the wall, press the towel stamp onto the wall to make an impression. Randomly alternate stamping different-colored squares across the wall in horizontal rows, occasionally applying multiple colors to the same square for interest.

STEEL REINFORCEMENTS

GO FOR A CLEAN, SLIGHTLY INDUSTRIAL FEEL with look-alike steel paneled walls created using a brush and rub technique. Base-coat wall with silver paint and let dry. Mask off 2-foot by 4-foot panels with painters tape. Using a nearly dry brush, quickly swipe a small amount of dark gray paint over the silver on each panel. Brush on a little more gray paint and wipe over it with a clean rag to soften. Remove tape and let dry. Outline each panel using a medium-tip black permanent marker and straight edge. To highlight the panels and create depth, dip a 4" putty knife into white paint and dab it just below the black marker lines at the top of each panel and along the right sides of the lines between panels. Let dry. Use a small hammer to pound silver upholstery tacks around each panel for a more realistic look.

SPATTERED *Stone*

FOR A SPECKLED WALL that suggests weathered stone, employ spray bottles, sponges and paintbrushes to apply glazes. It's a messy technique, so be sure to protect nearby surfaces. Base-coat wall with off-white latex paint. Let dry. In separate containers, mix equal amounts of glaze base with beige, olive, pale yellow and warm yellow latex paints. Pour the mixtures into individual spray bottles. Check to make sure the nozzles release a slight spattering of glaze. Work on one wall at a time, starting at the ceiling and moving downward. Lightly spray one color randomly over the wall (see photo). (Use a light touch—you can go over an area several times to achieve the desired effect.) Vary your distance from the wall to create different-size speckles. Try to minimize the streaks and runs; having a few will add to the effect, but too many can be distracting. To stop a drip, dab lightly with paper towel. Continue with the other color mixtures as above. If coverage in one area seems too heavy, let dry, then dab over it with a sea sponge loaded with white paint, turning the sponge as you work. Use a spattering technique to fill in sparse areas by dipping a chip brush into the desired color mixture and dragging the handle of an artist brush across the bristles to produce paint flecks.

Stand about 18 inches from the wall for this technique, but vary the distance to change the size of the spatter. Reload the brush as needed. If using more than one color, let the first dry before moving to the next. As you work, step back from the wall to check color and pattern balance.

AGED CRACKLE

A CRACKLE TREATMENT over brass metallic paint produces an elegantly aged effect with neoclassic appeal. With a paint roller, apply two coats of brass metallic paint to the wall. Let dry overnight. Apply two coats of crackle medium using a 6" roller. Let crackle dry following manufacturer's instructions. Apply a sandy-textured product with a steel trowel. Use a spatula to place the textured paint on the trowel's edge. Hold the trowel on an angle, with one side touching the wall, and smooth the sandstone onto the wall, leaving random spaces uncovered to reveal the brass paint below. When using a trowel, work away from corners, down from the ceiling and up from chair rail or baseboard. The textured paint will separate to form cracks as it dries. When the paint is dry, mix brass metallic paint with glaze base and apply over the treatment with a chip brush.

TALK *about Texture*

IF YOUR WALLS ARE LESS THAN PERFECT, don't despair. There's no need to hide them with wallpaper or replace your drywall—just treat them to a new texture. Because texture treatments are variable by nature, any wall irregularities are easily camouflaged. You can achieve a textured look either by applying a dimensional medium, like Venetian plaster or a stone compound, or by creating the appearance of texture through the application of paint, such as dry brushing or ragging.

TWO-TONE *Layering*

1. Pour strawberry paint into one half of the paint tray and light tan paint into the other so the colors are side by side (see photo A). (Start with a small amount of each color to minimize the possibility of mixing together, adding more paint to the tray as needed.)

2. Move the roller into the paint so that it picks up each color, with one color on each side, touching in the center of the roller.

3. Working on an approximately 4-foot by 4-foot section of wall at a time, apply the paint to the wall using short strokes, varying the direction of the roller (see photo B). You will not need to apply much pressure because the long nap of the roller will help spread the paint. Do not overwork the paint; the longer you roll the paint, the more blended the colors will be.

4. Turn the roller over and continue to work on the same section, blending the colors together. (Turning the roller over allows for a more even application of the two colors.)

5. Continue going over the section to blend and soften the colors until you are satisfied with the look (see photo C).

6. Move on to the next section and repeat the technique to blend edges into the adjacent area. As you finish each section, step back from the wall to check the overall effect.

SHOPPING LIST

- Flat latex paint in strawberry and light tan
- Paint tray
- ¾"-nap masonry roller cover

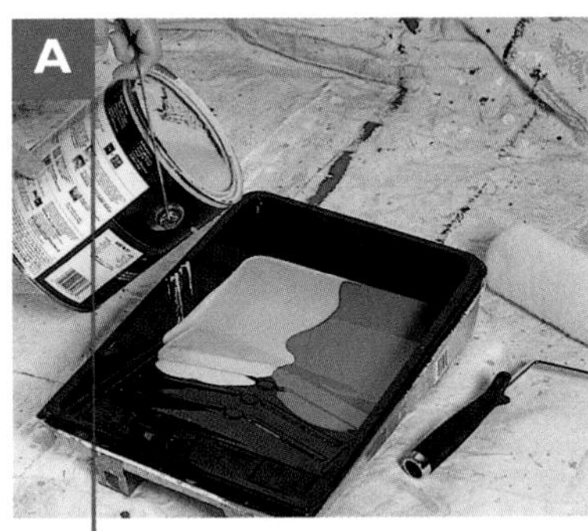
A

B

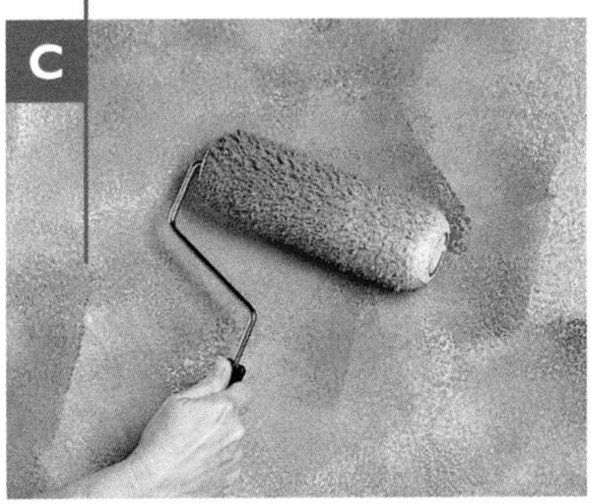
C

MARBLED GLAZE

YOU CAN ACHIEVE OTHER EFFECTS using different colors of paint or glaze in the same paint tray. For these glowing golden walls, start with a sunny yellow base coat. Fill the deep pan of a paint tray with glaze base. Next, randomly pour sunflower yellow premixed colored glaze onto the clear glaze. Gently draw a paint stick through the mixture in several places so it has a slightly marbled look. (Do not completely blend the glazes or the random color variation will not occur.) As you use up the glaze mixture, add more of each glaze, as needed, to the paint tray. Dab a ½"-nap roller into the mixture, being sure to gather both clear and colored glazes. Apply the roller randomly to the wall, spreading the glazes widely within arm's reach. Leave some areas of the base coat peeking through. Holding a standard foam roller in your other hand, lightly smooth and blend areas with concentrated glaze. In other areas, use a soft rag to gently lift off glaze, revealing more of the base coat and imprinting the cloth texture. If desired, finish the just-glazed area by wiping the rag across the wall surface to create highlights.

CHEESECLOTH *Imprints*

1. Pick two different shades of the same color. We chose dark sage and light celery. Measure and mark a level line at chair rail height on the wall. Base-coat the bottom of the wall (up to chair rail height) with the darker color and the upper portion of the wall with the lighter color. Let dry.

2. Unfold and cut a piece of cheesecloth about 2 feet long and the same height as the painted area below the chair rail (about 36 inches). Temporarily secure the corners of the cheesecloth to a large piece of scrap cardboard using thumbtacks. This protects your work surface while you apply paint to the cheesecloth.

3. Pour the lighter paint color into your paint tray. (Wear gloves for the remainder of this paint technique.) Using a short-nap foam paint roller, coat cheesecloth with paint (see photo A).

4. Peel the cheesecloth off of the cardboard, keeping a few thumbtacks in hand, and tack it to the lower portion of the wall (see photo B). (You may wish to work with a partner for this portion of the technique for ease of handling the painted cloth.) Cover with a plastic drop cloth and flatten it against the wall with a clean paint roller or by patting it with your hands (see photo C).

5. Gently peel off the plastic and cheesecloth. Continue around the room, overlapping each cheesecloth impression by a few inches. Experiment with cheesecloth application by draping it, pulling it taut or applying a second coat to achieve variation in the finish. Let dry.

6. Stain, cut and install pine chair rail molding over the seam where the two paint colors meet on the wall.

SHOPPING LIST

- Flat latex paint in dark sage and light celery
- Yardstick level
- Pencil
- Cheesecloth
- Scissors
- Cardboard
- Thumbtacks
- Rubber gloves
- Short-nap foam roller
- Paint tray
- Plastic drop cloth
- Standard paint roller and cover
- Pine chair rail molding
- Light-toned water-based wood stain

A

B

C

OTHER IMPRESSIONS

HERE WE USED AN INEXPENSIVE household item—cheesecloth—to create interesting wrinkles and folds in wet paint. This technique is similar to frottage (see bubble-wrap stripes, page 87). Experiment with other types of fibers to produce additional striking textured effects. Try using pieces of terry cloth toweling, crumpled cotton rags, waffle-weave fabric or even newspaper to give walls a uniquely textured appearance.

FLOWERING KALE
basil

FADED PLAID *Dry Brush*

SHOPPING LIST

- Flat latex paint in gray-green and white
- Metallic paint in opaque champagne
- 2" and 4" paintbrushes
- Paper towels

1. Base-coat wall with gray-green paint. Let dry.

2. Dip the tips of the bristles of a 4" paintbrush into white paint and dab off excess onto a paper towel. Starting at any point on the wall, use light pressure to create a vertical stripe-like brush stroke, pulling the brush downward until it runs out of paint (see photo A).

3. Before the paint dries, feather the edges of the stripe outward to soften it and create small, faint, horizontal stripes by brushing across it (see photo B).

4. Working on one small section at a time, continue to dry brush vertical and horizontal stripes to create a pattern that resembles pieced-together scraps of plaid. Be sure to drag the brush across the stripes to soften the edges as above. Alternate the vertical and horizontal application to ensure balance in the overall effect. You do not want the wall to look like it has either strong vertical or horizontal lines. (We intended for it to look like a faded plaid, and this is achieved by softening each brush stroke and allowing the green base coat to show through.) Continue until entire wall is complete. Let dry.

5. Load a 2" brush with opaque champagne-colored metallic paint, wipe excess on paper towel and apply to random sections as above to add more visual texture (see photo C). Let dry.

A

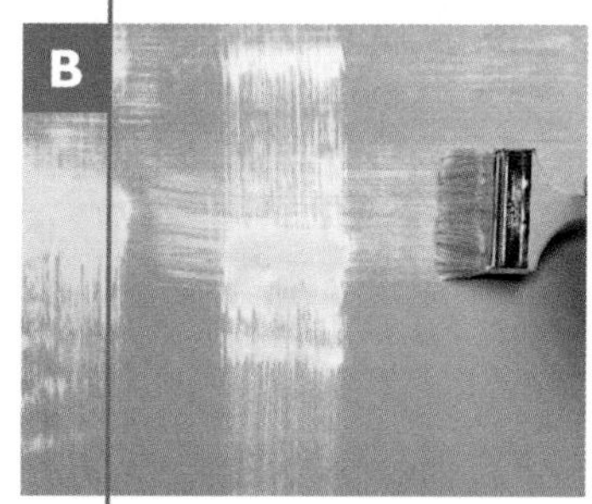
B

C

SINGULAR SENSATION

DRY BRUSHING WITH ONE COLOR can produce a dramatic look as well—here, we used yellow paint over a white base coat. Lightly dip the bristles of a wide paintbrush into yellow paint and wipe excess on a paper towel or plate. Apply the paint in various directions, making it heavier in some areas and fanning out the edges until you have used all the paint on the brush. Reload the brush and continue. When painting in this freeform style, be sure the overall appearance is balanced by stepping back occasionally to view the wall from a distance. Continue painting until wall is covered.

NO STONE *Unturned*

CREATE GROOVES IN STONE MEDIUM with a slight sheen to mimic the look of cement or textured ceramics on your walls. Base-coat the wall with pale gray flat paint. Let dry. Use a Japan scraper to spread an even coat of stone medium onto the wall in 4-foot by 4-foot sections. Smooth the stone medium with the scraper to create a fairly flat surface. Determine whether the grooves will be horizontal or vertical. Hold the scraper so that the edge of the tool will create the groove imprint in the determined direction. Tap the tip or edge of the scraper into the medium to create a groove or line imprint, moving across the wall either horizontally or vertically, depending on your determined direction (see photo).

Continue creating rows of grooves until the section is complete. (The medium does not dry immediately so there is room for error. If you make a mistake, use the scraper to smooth over it and try again.) Continue applying the medium to 4-foot by 4-foot sections, blending the edges of one section into the next until the wall is complete. Let dry.

MEDITERRANEAN VISTA

TEXTURED LIMEWASH recreates the look of European country walls. Base-coat the wall with flat bluebell-colored paint. Let dry. Using a paint roller with a textured cover, apply textured limewash finish over the base coat, working in approximately 4-foot by 4-foot sections. Apply the limewash randomly, allowing much of the base coat to show through. Limewash dries in about 10 minutes; do not let it dry completely before the next step. Gently slide a taping knife down the limewash surface, knocking down the tips of the stipple left by the textured roller. Blend adjacent sections together before the limewash dries to avoid lines. Continue working in 4-foot by 4-foot sections, applying limewash and lightly scraping with the taping knife until the wall is complete. Allow to dry overnight. Finish by applying one to two coats of satin-finish sealer.

CREATIVE CROSSHATCHING

IF YOU HAVE WALLS WITH FLAWS, this softly textured treatment will hide them with ease. Use a roller to base-coat wall with satin-finish paint in sage. Let dry. With a dry paintbrush, apply off-white paint in a random crisscross pattern all over the wall, blotting the brush after each application to keep white transparent. Create areas with both heavy and light coverage. Let dry. Soak fine steel wool in denatured alcohol and rub across the wall to roughen the surface and break down the off-white paint for a softer look. (Wear gloves and safety glasses when applying denatured alcohol.) Use a cotton rag to apply paste wax to the wall, working in small sections. This gives the finish a soft sheen. When the wax is dry, buff with a clean, dry cloth.

VENETIAN *Plaster*

THIS FINISH OWES ITS TIME-CARESSED ELEGANCE to layers of a specialty paint product that you burnish and polish after application. Base-coat wall with flat latex paint in a goldenrod hue. Let dry. We chose this color because it matches our Venetian plaster color. Use a stainless-steel Japan scraper to apply Venetian plaster (a compound with the consistency of creamy peanut butter) to the wall, spreading a thin layer using swirling strokes (see photo). Work in approximately 2-foot sections. Let dry. Using 220-grit sandpaper, sand the surface in a circular motion to remove bumps and rough spots (see photo). Buff the wall with a clean, soft cloth. Each time you apply another layer of the marble, repeat the sanding and buffing process. We applied two layers. Each layer adds depth to the treatment. With the metal scraper, burnish your final surface using circular motions. The more pressure you use, the shinier the surface will become.

SAVVY *Stripes*

STRIPES COME IN ALL TYPES, from big and bold to slim and trim. And for as many kinds as there are, there are about as many different ways to make them. Start with a tried-and-true taping method, where you measure and mask off each stripe, or, for a less precise look, simply use the width of a paint roller as your stripe width. Make stripes from torn wallpaper or with metallic paint. Try them vertical or horizontal, opaque, transparent or somewhere in between—you're sure to find a style to suit any space.

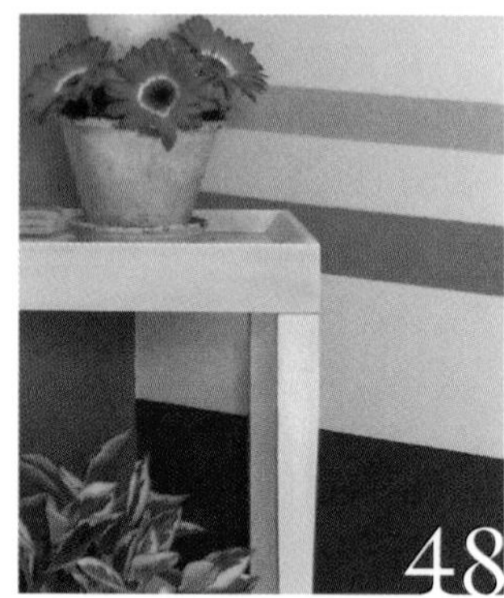

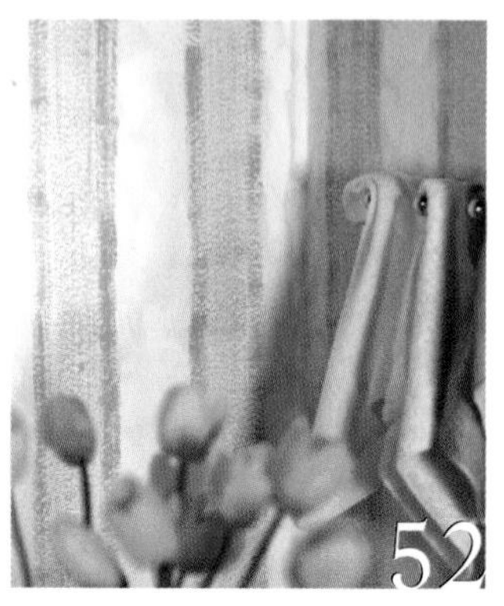

STRIPE AND STENCIL PAIRINGS

THIS TREATMENT FEATURES mottled glazes and dry brushing to create a look of timeworn elegance. For another way to combine stencils and stripes, but with a crisper look, pick two variations of the same color, such as light and dark lavender. Base-coat the wall with the lighter color and let dry. Next, measure, mark and tape off 2-foot-wide vertical stripes and paint every other stripe with the darker color. Pick a small stencil motif, such as a rosebud or leaf, and randomly stencil on the lighter stripes using the darker color.

AGING *Gracefully*

1. Base-coat wall with coral paint. Let dry.

2. Mix two parts gold paint with one part glaze. With a foam roller, apply the mixture to the wall, working in a 2-foot-square section.

3. While paint is still wet, roll vigorously with 1½"-nap rollers to blend and soften glaze, leaving some of the base color visible (see photo A). Continue across wall, working in 2-foot-square sections. As you work, step back occasionally to make sure that the treatment is consistent. Let dry for several hours. (If you add too much gold glaze mixture, lightly blend the base-coat color back over it.)

4. Determine placement of stencil and stripes. For our walls, we created a grouping of stripes—one 2-inch green stripe centered between two 1-inch gold stripes, with 1 inch between each stripe—to alternate with rows of stenciled flowers. Allowing 8 inches in between each group creates an elegant and balanced look. Begin planning the treatment at the center of the room, arranging the spacing so that the stencil does not end up in the corner, which would be difficult to paint. (Wall size varies; alter spacing to work out evenly for your walls.) Use a pencil and yardstick level to mark vertical placement guidelines on the wall.

5. If you wish to make your own stencil, draw the pattern on acetate with a fine-point black permanent marker and cut out using a heated stencil-cutting tool or craft knife. (We cut several stencil sheets and taped them together to create a continuous pattern to apply to the wall.) If you are reusing one stencil sheet, be sure to use consistent spacing.

6. Place stencil on wall, centering it over a vertical guideline. We positioned ours so a flower rested just above the baseboard. Mark the center of one of the flowers on the wall. Transfer this alignment around the room on the vertical guidelines, using a pencil and a yardstick level, to ensure alignment of stencil from row to row. Indicate your placement flower by marking it on the stencil. As you begin to stencil each row of flowers, align the center of this flower with the marked horizontal guidelines.

7. Use painters tape or stencil adhesive to secure the stencil in place. Apply gold to the flowers and green to the stems with a makeup sponge (see photo B). Complete row and continue around the room, stenciling each row on the marked guidelines.

8. Use an artist brush to accent the center of each flower with a crescent of pale yellow paint (see photo C).

9. Create the 2-inch green stripes by lightly dragging a mostly dry 2" brush down the wall, centering it over the marked guidelines. (The stripes need not be precise—variations and imperfections contribute to the softly aged look of the treatment.) Continue around the room until all of the green stripes are finished.

10. Using a 1" brush and gold paint, repeat the dry-brushed effect to create a 1-inch stripe on each side of the green stripes, leaving 1 inch between each stripe (see photo D). Let dry.

SHOPPING LIST

- Flat latex paint in coral, gold and sage
- Glaze base
- Foam roller
- 1½"-nap paint roller
- Simple scrolled flower stencil or acetate, fine-point permanent marker and heated stencil-cutting tool or craft knife
- Painters tape or stencil adhesive
- Yardstick level
- Wedge-shaped makeup sponges
- Acrylic craft paint in pale yellow
- Artist brush
- 1" and 2" paintbrushes

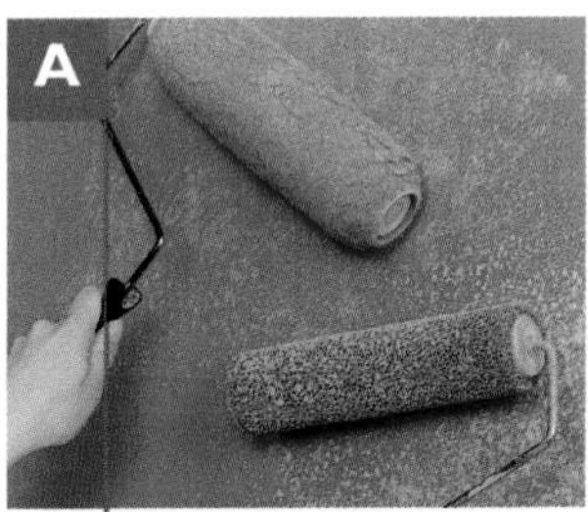
A

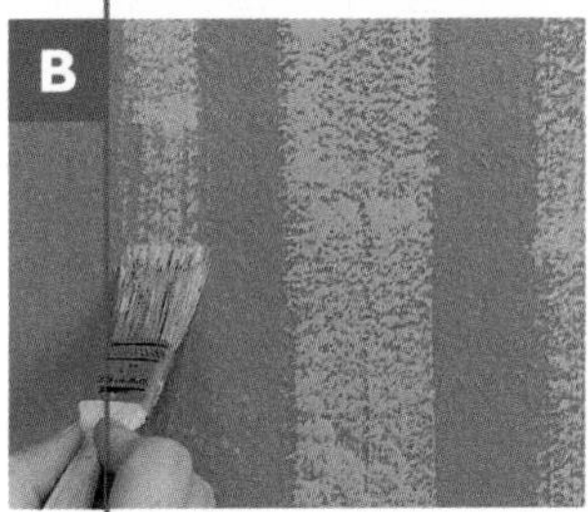
B

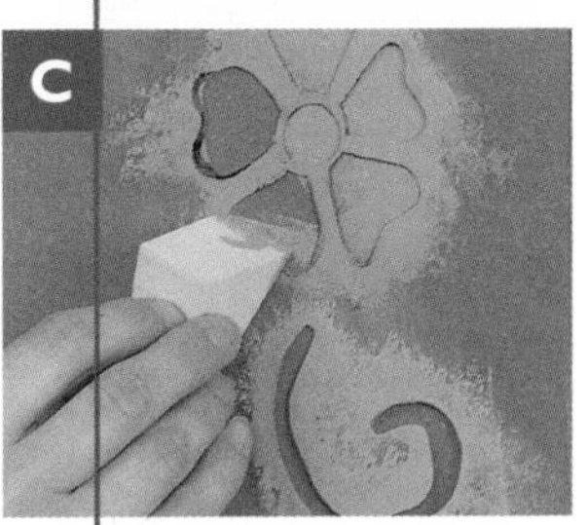
C

D

MOCHA *Magic*

1. Base-coat wall with pale pink paint. Let dry.

2. Plan stripe layout on the wall by starting at the baseboard. (To create our stripe design, we painted a 6-inch stripe in chocolate brown, followed by a 6-inch space. Then, we placed a 3-inch cocoa stripe above that, followed by a 3-inch space. We finished with a 2-inch stripe in latte.) Plan to repeat the same pattern in reverse at the top of the wall.

3. Place the 6" template along the baseboard and level. Apply a strip of 1½" painters tape along template's top edge to mask the first stripe. Remove the stripe template from the wall and continue around the wall in the same manner. Apply additional spray adhesive when needed. The area beneath the tape guideline will be painted chocolate brown.

4. Measure up 6 inches from the bottom of the tape edge, leaving a space that will remain pink. You may want to mark area with a small X of tape to remind yourself not to apply paint here. Apply the 3" template and level. Press into place. Apply tape along top and bottom edges of template. The area between the two pieces of tape will be the 3-inch cocoa stripe. Continue around the entire wall.

5. Measure up 3 inches from the bottom of the last tape guideline, leaving a space, which will remain pink. Apply the 2" template and level. Press into place. Place a strip of painters tape along the top and bottom edges of the template. Remove the template and continue around the room (see photo A). (Don't worry about marking the 3-inch pale pink space because it will be covered up with two strips of 1½" tape.)

6. Repeat the taping process at the top of the wall. Depending on your ceiling style/height and room features, you may want to adjust stripe placement. We planned our stripes so the bottom of the top stripe aligns with the top of our French doors.

7. When everything has been taped off, use a sponge brush or paint roller to apply the various paint colors to the stripes (see photo B). Work on one color at a time, applying two coats of paint and then removing tape immediately. Move onto the next color and continue in this manner until the entire wall is finished. Let dry.

SHOPPING LIST

- Flat latex paint in pale pink, chocolate brown, cocoa and latte
- Stripe templates in 6", 3" and 2" widths
- Repositionable spray adhesive
- Yardstick level
- 1½" painters tape
- Paint trays and liners
- Paint rollers or sponge brushes

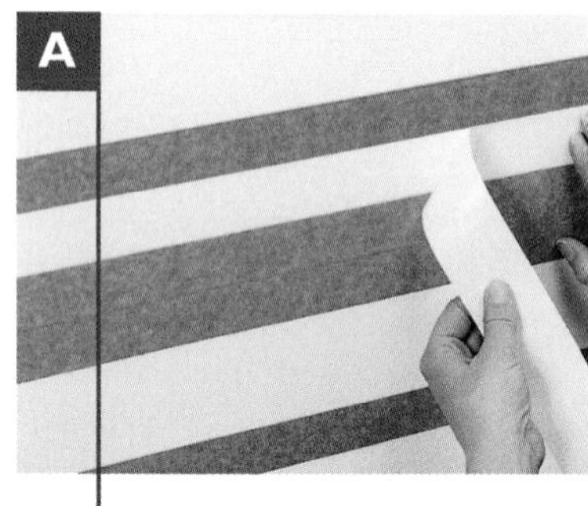
A

B

SPEEDY STRIPING

USE STRIPE TEMPLATES as helpful guides when masking a wall to paint stripes. To stick a stripe template to wall, spray the back with adhesive. Check that the template is straight with a yardstick level. When using the template to mask a stripe, you can tape on either side. The template can also be used to mask a space, but you will have to draw a pencil guideline following the template's edge and apply tape to the guideline after removing the template.

REMNANT RESCUE:

IF YOU'RE A BARGAIN-SAVVY DECORATOR, chances are you've rummaged the remnant bin at your local wallcoverings store or home center. Maybe you picked out a pattern you liked but had more wall to cover than paper available. This treatment, which uses ripped lengths of paper in one or more patterns to create a striped wall, is the perfect solution. We paired toile and paisley papers in reds and yellows, but you can achieve a similar look with more than two compatible papers in any colorway.

TASTEFULLY *Tattered*

PREPARATION

1. Pick a base-coat color to match your wallpaper background and paint wall. Let dry.

2. Measure wall to determine the approximate width of each strip of ripped wallpaper and spacing between strips. (Our strips were 7 to 10 inches wide, with 3 and 5 inches between strips. Our rolls of wallpaper were 27 inches wide, so we were able to rip three strips per width of each roll. The 9 yards of paper on each roll yielded enough strips to cover our 8-foot by 8-foot wall, with plenty to spare.)

3. Partially unroll wallpaper. Place a weight at each end to keep the paper flat. At desired width, slowly begin to tear a strip (see photo A). Do not try to make the ripped edge of the strip straight; allow the strip width to vary slightly to add interest. The strip should be several inches longer than your wall height; you will cut away excess later. Tear strips from both wallpaper patterns until you have enough for your wall.

4. Temporarily tape the alternating patterned strips on the wall and adjust spacing and pattern alignment until satisfied, working on one wall at a time. This treatment allows room for error; you can adjust the spacing, especially in the corners.

5. To ensure strips will be straight, select a motif that repeats down the length of each strip as a reference. Because the patterns will vary from strip to strip, you will have to choose a new repeating motif for each strip. To measure and mark the first set of vertical guidelines corresponding to the repeating motifs, start from the corner of the room and measure out to the selected motif on the first strip. Transfer that mark to the wall and remove the strip. From the marked point, extend a line down the wall using a yardstick level and pencil.

6. Using the first line as a reference, measure out to the selected motif on the next strip. Remove the strip and repeat the process of marking a guideline on the wall (see photo B). To avoid confusing the strips and motif placement, hang the previous strip after you finish marking the placement for the next strip; see Hanging the Strips instructions. As you work across a wall, alternate between marking a new line and hanging the corresponding strip over the previous guideline. Make sure patterned papers alternate all the way around the room.

HANGING THE STRIPS

1. Lay strip on a flat surface. With a brush, apply wallcovering adhesive following manufacturer's instructions.

2. Hang strip on wall, aligning the motif repeat over the marked guideline (see photo C). Allow excess paper to extend past the top and bottom of the wall.

3. With a wallpaper brush, press out excess paste and air bubbles, wiping away paste with a damp rag.

4. Use a straightedge and a craft knife to trim excess paper at the top and bottom of the wall. When all the strips are hung, let dry overnight.

5. Mix one part white paint with two or three parts glaze to make a milky wash. With a paintbrush, apply mixture to the wall in small sections. While glaze is still wet, blend into the wall with a rag (see photo D). Continue until you have covered the entire wall.

SHOPPING LIST

- Flat latex paint in light shade to coordinate with background of wallpaper
- Two coordinating wallpaper patterns
- Prepasted wallcovering adhesive
- Yardstick level
- Straightedge
- Paintbrushes
- Wallpaper brush
- Latex or acrylic paint in white
- Glaze base
- Rags or towels
- Craft knife

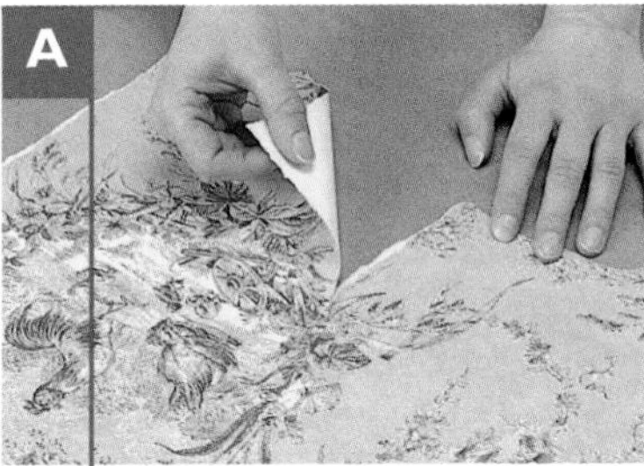
A

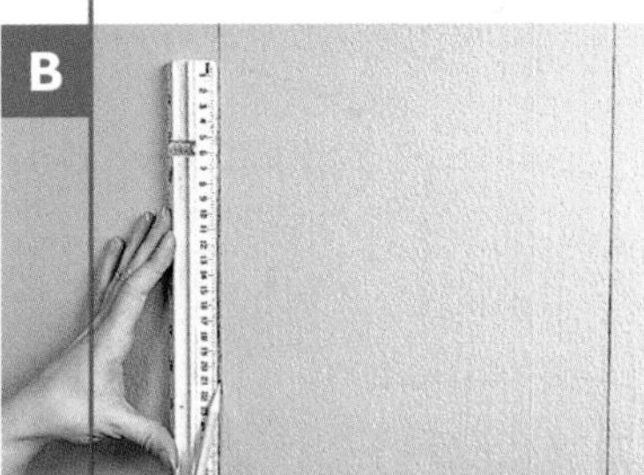
B

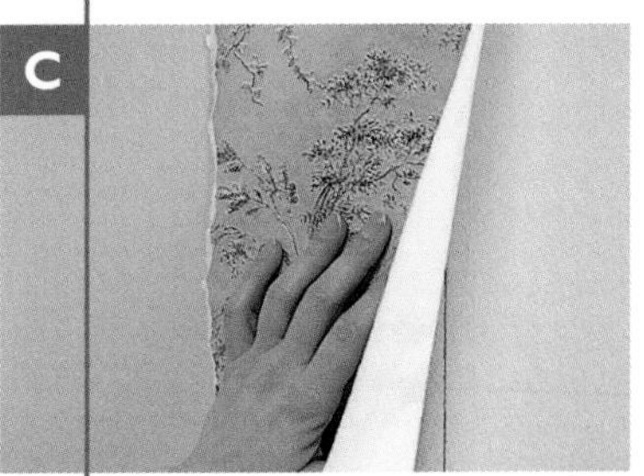
C

D

PERFECTLY *Pastel*

1. Base-coat the wall with vanilla paint and let dry.

2. Determine width of stripes. (We used a 1-inch green stripe, a 2-inch blue stripe, another 1-inch green stripe and a 3-inch cream stripe that was dry brushed with white. We repeated this pattern across the wall.)

3. Use a level and colored pencil to mark stripe lines extending from just under the ceiling to the floor. Select a colored pencil the same color as your stripes for marking lines; after you paint, the lines won't be visible. We marked off 2-inch-wide stripes with a blue colored pencil, leaving 5 inches in between to allow for the green and cream stripes.

4. Mix one part blue paint with one part glaze. Dip a 2" paintbrush in the mixture, wiping some excess onto a paper towel. Lightly brush paint down the 2-inch stripes, allowing some base color to show through while varying the thickness of the paint (see photo A). Let dry.

5. Mix one part green paint with one part glaze. Dip a 1" paintbrush in the mixture, wiping some excess onto a paper towel. Apply a green stripe on either side of the blue as above. Maintain the width of the stripe as close to 1 inch as possible, using the brush width as your guide (see photo B). Let dry.

6. There will be a 3-inch stripe remaining in between the green stripes. Apply white paint to a 1½" paintbrush as above. Paint over the vanilla base coat in this area, varying the width and direction of the paint strokes. Apply paint more heavily in some areas, allowing the base color to show through (see photo C). Let dry.

SHOPPING LIST

- Painters tape
- Flat latex paint in bright blue, grass green, vanilla and pure white
- Glaze base
- Blue colored pencil
- 36" level
- 1", 1½" and 2" paintbrushes
- Paper towel

A

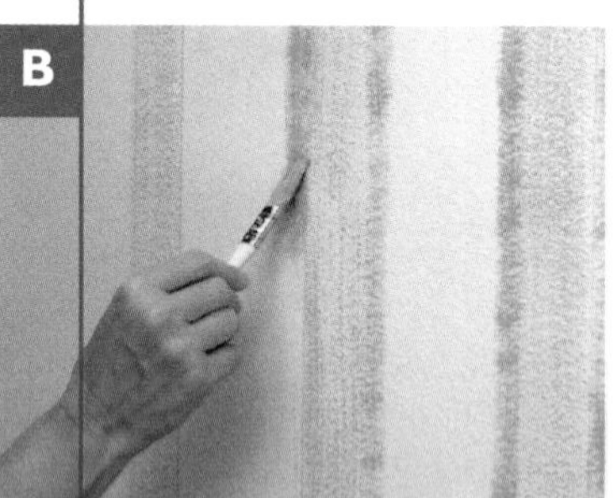
B

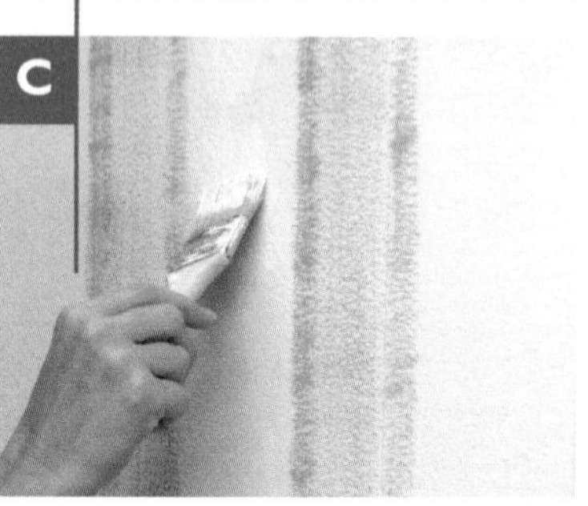
C

ARTISTIC INSPIRATION

LOOK TO A FAVORITE ARTWORK FOR INSPIRATION when devising a paint treatment. You might use it to help pick color choices, motifs or the method of application. Here a whimsical print of a couple tending to flowers and pets on their balcony led us to create wall stripes with the same sketchbook-pastel quality. We used various widths of paintbrushes and thin glazes of color to create the stripes. Because we did not mask off the stripes with tape, the edges are not precise, giving the treatment a softer look. Elsewhere in the room, we copied the flower shapes to stamp on the shower curtain and the ceramic sink, further linking the room decor to the art print.

SILVER *Shimmers*

THIS GLEAMING TECHNIQUE created with a paint pad and metallic paint looks great on both textured and smooth walls. Base-coat wall with flat periwinkle paint. Let dry. (Cool colors, such as blues, greens and purples, work well with metallics. The metallic paint stands out better on darker shades.) Measure wall and determine stripe width. The width of the stripes should be at least as wide as your pad painter. We used a 7" paint pad and made 9-inch stripes. Center your first stripe over the midline of the wall, marking the ceiling and baseboard with a pencil. Measure and mark the stripe pattern on the rest of the wall, working from the center out to the corners. Snap chalk lines from the floor to the ceiling at the marked points. With a paintbrush, lightly apply opaque silver metallic paint to the pad painter surface. (If you dip the pad into the paint, it becomes saturated and looks too thick when applied to the wall.) Starting at the top of the wall at the first marked stripe, lightly drag the paint pad downward within the chalk outline. Vary the pressure slightly as you paint for a more irregular look. If the stripe is wider than the pad, first align the pad with the left chalk line and drag it down the wall, then go back to the top and align it with the right chalk line and drag down the wall again. Paint all stripes in the same manner and let dry.

TONE ON TONE

FOR A SUBTLE STRIPED EFFECT, pair eggshell paint with clear sealer. To begin, base-coat wall with paint in an eggshell finish. Here, we used a soft lavender color. When the paint is dry, use a tape measure, pencil and straight edge to measure and mark placement of evenly spaced stripes (ours were 2 inches) all around the room, making adjustments, if needed, at corners. Mask off the stripes with high-tack painters tape. (It may help to apply tape as a team, with one person on a ladder lining up the tape with the top marks and the other stretching it to the floor and checking to make sure it is straight.) Working on just a few rows at a time, apply a water-based clear-coat sealer to the masked-off stripes using a small foam roller. Remove the tape around the stripes you have just painted to prevent seepage of the polyurethane, then continue across the wall as above.

COLOR OUTSIDE

STRIPES NEEDN'T ALWAYS BE CRISPLY EDGED, as this softly textured treatment proves. Base-coat wall with pale yellow paint. Let dry. Determine stripe width and spacing. We created groups of three 2-inch pink stripes separated by 1-inch stripes of the base-coat color. The entire stripe grouping is 8 inches wide, with 6 inches between each set. Adjust the total width of your stripe groupings to best fit your wall. Starting at the center of a wall, use a pencil and yardstick level to mark the first vertical stripe guideline. To quickly mark the rest of the stripes in that grouping, use the marked guidelines on a transparent quilters ruler. Recheck stripes with level as you go. Make spacing adjustments at the corners of the room, if needed. Apply painters tape to the outside edge of each stripe grouping, then apply 1" tape to mask off the narrower stripes between the 2-inch stripes. Pour strawberry pink paint into a lined paint tray. Dip a crumpled white plastic bag (without printing—ink may transfer to the wall) into the pink paint, picking up a small amount. Move the bag around to evenly distribute the paint. Apply the paint over the taped-off 2" stripes in a random fashion, beginning at the top of the wall and moving down. Portions of the base coat should remain visible. Move the bag around to use paint from all parts of the bag and add more paint as needed (see photo). Begin by bagging lightly over an area and slowly add more paint until satisfied. Don't worry if small amounts of paint get into areas between the stripes; this will be blended with more pink paint to create the textured finish. Let dry. Continue around the room, painting all stripes. Switch to fresh bags when they become saturated. Remove all tape from wall. To make wall appear textured, smudged and worn, use a new bag to lightly apply patches of pink paint between the pink stripes and on top of the 6-inch base-coated stripes between stripe groupings. Blend paint over previously textured spots to eliminate paint lines. Complete the entire wall, working on one stripe grouping at a time.

STENCILS & Stamps

SOME FOLKS HAVE A NATURAL ability to render artful images with mere brushes and paints. For the rest of us, there are stamps and stencils. You'll find them available in hundreds of styles, shapes and sizes—or you can easily make your own. Though they're attractive for their uniformity, they don't have to be cookie-cutter creations—you can pair them with a variety of materials and easily added details for stunning results. Gold leafing, dimensional paint, wallpaper cutouts and more transform staid stencils and stamps into standouts.

SWAYING *Palms*

1. Base-coat wall with light yellow-green paint. Let dry.

2. Trace around the leaves on stencil acetate with a fine-point permanent marker (see photo A). Cut out leaf shapes with a craft knife or the stencil-cutting point of a heat stencil-cutting tool. Use acetate leaf shapes for reverse stenciling technique. Save other acetate pieces, with leaves cut out, for traditional stenciling in areas like the chair-rail border.

3. Use a yardstick level and white chalk to mark a horizontal guideline 36 inches from the floor for the chair-rail border. Spray the back of the lemon-leaf stencil with adhesive spray and press the stencil onto the center of the wall just above the chalk line.

4. Pour a small amount of each paint color onto a foam plate. Lightly dab a makeup sponge into dark leaf green paint. With a pouncing motion, apply paint to the wall, starting at the outside edge of the stencil and working inward. Add touches of medium lime green and light leaf green paints with fresh makeup sponges for shading. Repeat stencil around the room, following chalk guideline and placing leaves approximately 2 inches apart. You may need to adjust the spacing of the stencil near the corners of the room to ensure the border is evenly made up of whole leaves. For visual interest, alternate orientation of stencil so every other leaf is placed with the stem up. Let dry. Wipe away chalk guideline with damp paper towel.

TIP: *Use paper leaf cutouts to help plan placement of leaves on your walls. Trace leaf shapes onto paper and make desired number of copies, then cutout. Tape paper leaf shapes to the wall using painters tape to create a pleasing arrangement. Remove paper leaves as you paint.*

5. Plan placement of reverse-stenciled leaves on the wall above the chair-rail border so there is a balanced composition of colors, sizes and shapes. Leaves should be placed in varying directions with a few overlapping. Use dark leaf green paint for lemon, magnolia and philodendron leaves, medium leaf green for large galax leaves, light leaf green for Japanese aralia and medium lime green for small galax and peace lily leaves.

6. Begin with the largest leaf. Spray the back of leaf shape with stencil adhesive and place on the wall in the desired location. Dip a ½" bristle brush in paint, wiping excess paint on paper towel. Lightly brush paint out from the shape's edge onto wall the outline will show brush strokes (see photo B). Repeat in other spots on the wall. Let dry.

7. Spray the back of a large galax leaf shape with stencil adhesive and position on the wall. Dab a makeup sponge into the paint. Wipe the excess paint on a paper towel. Lightly pounce the sponge around the edge of the leaf shape to create a leaf outline (see photo C). Repeat in other spots on the wall. Let dry.

8. Repeat the reverse stenciling using other leaf shapes and paint colors on the walls. Alternate the sponging technique and the brushing technique to create a mix of textured outlines. Step back occasionally to check that the design looks balanced and add different colors, leaf shapes or sizes as needed. Let dry.

9. Using an artist brush and matching paint colors, add veining to the reverse-stenciled leaves.

10. For interest and color balance, add a few solid lemon and magnolia leaves using the chair-rail technique. Let dry.

11. Protect with a clear matte sealer.

SHOPPING LIST

- Flat latex paint in light yellow-green, dark leaf green, medium lime green, light leaf green and medium leaf green
- Assorted tropical leaves, such as lemon, magnolia, peace lily, two sizes of galax, philodendron and Japanese aralia
- Stencil acetate
- Fine-point permanent marker
- Craft knife or heat stencil-cutting tool
- Yardstick level
- White chalk
- Stencil adhesive spray
- Foam plate
- Wedge-shaped makeup sponges
- ½" bristle brushes
- Artist brushes
- Clear matte sealer
- Paper towels

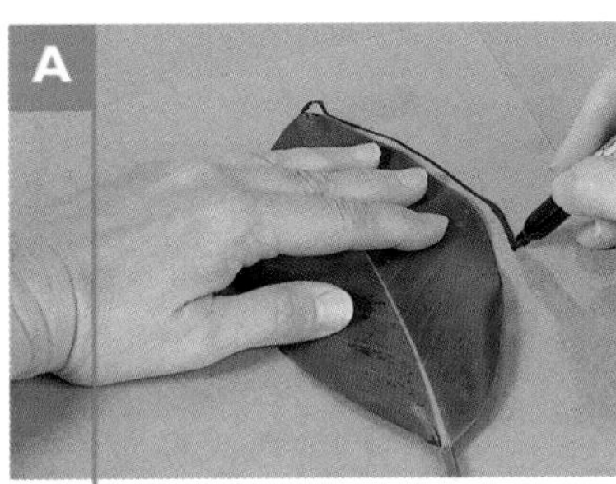
A

B

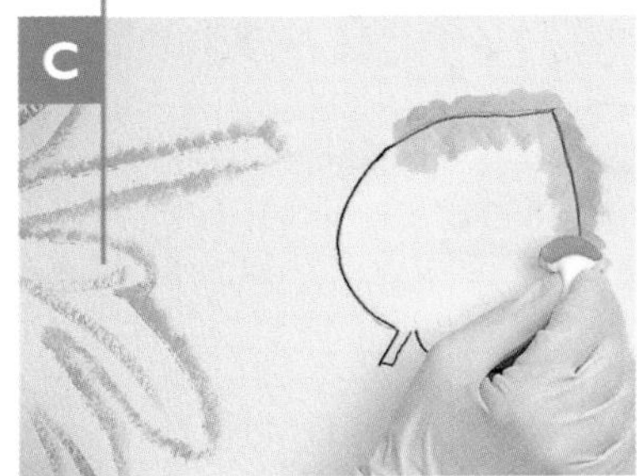
C

PAPER *Roses*

STENCILING

1. Base-coat wall with pale blue paint. Let dry.

2. Using a yardstick level and pencil, lightly mark a vertical line where you will start stenciling. Start at the top center of the room's focal wall and work outward toward the corners as you move around the room. (If you're doing an entire room, treat opposite walls as partners when planning your stencil placement. Adjust stencil designs at the room's corners. Stencil corners after walls are complete.)

3. Spray the back of the stencil sheet with adhesive. Line up registration holes on one side of stencil sheet with the vertical line. Press stencil against wall and pencil a mark through the top of each of the four registration holes. These marks ensure proper alignment when repositioning the stencil for the next row of stenciling.

4. Pour medium teal paint onto a foam plate. Dampen a sea sponge with water and wring out excess. Wearing rubber gloves, dip the sponge into the paint. Blot excess onto a paper towel. Lightly press the sponge over the stencil using a dabbing motion.

5. Move the stencil over to the next position. Line up the registration holes on one side of the stencil with the pencil marks from the previous stencil. Secure the stencil to the wall, make pencil marks through the opposite two holes and continue applying paint. Be careful not to smudge the paint as you move the stencil. To prevent this, wipe paint buildup from stencil sheet with a damp sponge. Continue working across the wall in vertical rows. Let paint dry overnight.

6. Place a small amount of light gray paint onto a foam plate. Dip a 1½" paintbrush into paint and wipe excess onto a paper towel. Lightly dry brush patches of paint onto some areas of the wall to give the stenciled patterns a worn and softer appearance (see photo A).

ADDING PAPER ACCENTS

1. Choose paper with flowers, leaves or other motifs sized to suit your stencil pattern.

2. Cut out motifs with scissors and determine placement and spacing on the wall. (We used 20 sheets of 12" x 12" scrapbook paper for our 8-foot by 8-foot wall.)

3. Apply wallpaper paste to the back of the flower cutouts with a damp sponge. Smooth the flowers on the wall with the sponge (see photo A). Use the sponge to work out bubbles and wipe away excess paste. Apply the leaves in the same manner.

4. Select areas of the stencil to highlight with paint. On a foam plate, thin paint with a few drops of water for smoother application.

5. Using an artist brush and thinned paint, add shading to selected areas of the stencil and embellish the wall with freehand details, like tendrils (see photo B). Let dry.

6. Using an artist brush, add highlights in a lighter color around the shading (see photo C). If needed, custom blend paint colors to match elements in your paper. Let dry.

SHOPPING LIST

- Flat latex paint in pale blue, medium teal and light gray
- Yardstick level
- Large-scale scroll-pattern stencil
- Repositionable spray adhesive
- Foam plates
- Sea sponge
- Rubber gloves
- Paper towels and clean, damp sponges
- 1½" paintbrush
- Scrapbook paper (we used 12" x 12" with large roses)
- Scissors
- Clear wallpaper adhesive
- Small artist brushes
- Acrylic craft paint in colors that coordinate with your wall, stencil and paper colors (we used yellow-green, pale yellow, white and leaf green)

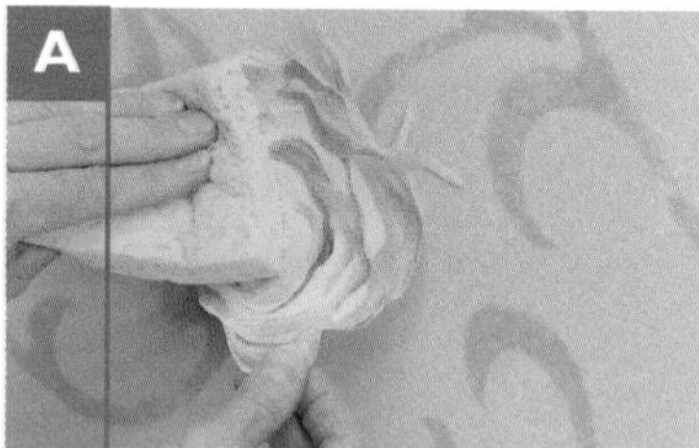
A

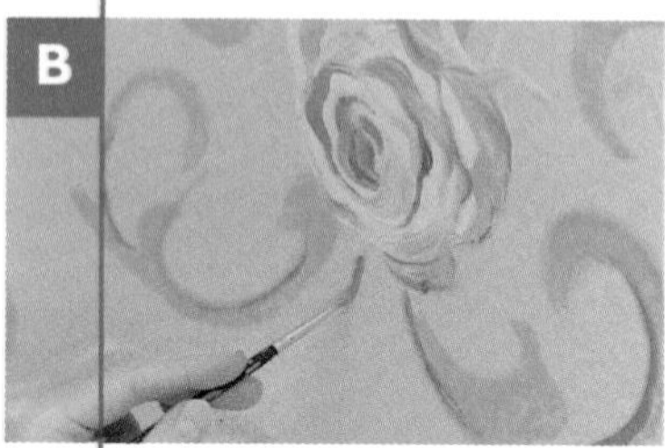
B

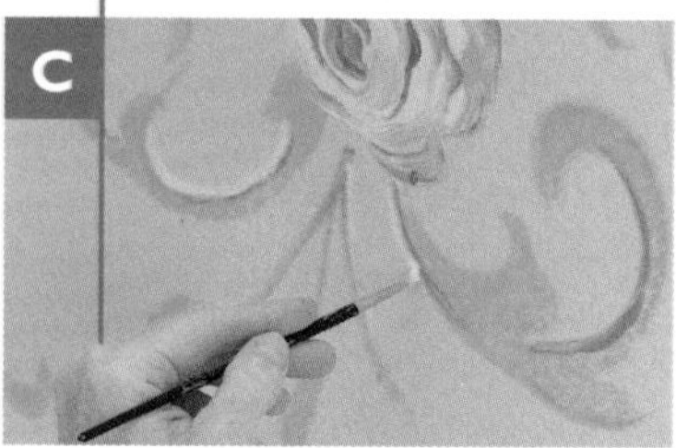
C

TIP: *Purchase two stencils. Buy one to use on flat portions of the wall and the other for bending into corners.*

EASY UPDATE

THIS IS A VERSITILE TREATMENT—you may choose to start with only the large allover stencil to mimic the look of custom handpainted wallpaper. When you're ready for a change, you can paint over it—or embellish it with paper accents and handpainted details to create a brand-new design. Clip cabbage roses or other big blooms from high-quality gift wrap, wallpaper or scrapbook paper, then brush on tendrils and stems. Or choose another motif and adjust the painted details accordingly; let your imagination be your guide.

CRAZY *for Daisies*

1. Base-coat wall with gray-brown paint. Let dry.

2. Determine the placement of flowers and mark on the wall with pencil. We used random spacing, placing flowers no closer than 12 inches apart for a more open effect.

3. With a small foam paintbrush, lightly apply white to the stamp (see photo A). (For another effect, try a contrasting or complementary color instead of white and tint the modeling paste to match.)

4. With a rocking motion, stamp the image onto the wall at marked points (see photo B). Continue until all flowers have been stamped onto the wall. Let dry. Vary the direction of the flower placement for interest.

5. Assemble cake bag with coupler and decorating tip.

6. Fill bag with modeling paste, being careful not to create air pockets in the bag. (Air pockets will cause the modeling paste to be discharged unevenly, disrupting the flow of the design.)

7. Apply modeling paste to outline one side of each petal and the center of the flower, gently squeezing the bag as you go (see photo C). Let dry. If the decorating tip becomes clogged, insert a straight pin into the opening to clear the blockage.

8. Squiggle a line to create a stem beneath each stamped flower. Let dry.

9. Create leaves on some stems as above to add interest to the design. Let dry. When you wish to change the wall treatment, simply scrape off and sand down the modeling paste until the wall is smooth.

SHOPPING LIST

- Flat latex paint in white and gray-brown
- Freeform flower rubber stamp
- Small foam paintbrush
- 12" cake-decorating bag and coupler
- #5 round decorating tip
- Modeling paste

TIP: *You can use different cake decorating tips to make more dimensional shapes with modeling paste. For example, try a star tip to create flower buds or a leaf tip to fashion different-sized foliage.*

SAVVY STAMPING

BESIDES A FOAM PAINTBRUSH, you can also use a wedge-shaped makeup sponge or a small roller to apply paint to the stamp.

- A little paint goes a long way on rubber stamps. To best highlight the design, take care to apply paint to only the raised portions of the stamp.
- Use a firm, even pressure to fully transfer your stamped design.

DIAMOND *in the Rough*

1. Base-coat the wall with gold paint.

2. Determine your pattern and the area to be painted. (For our walls, we created a dense design on the lower three-quarters of the wall, with a more open, random pattern on the remainder of the wall.) Decide how about high you want the dense pattern to go and deduct the baseboard height from that measurement. Measure the diagonal length of your tile stamp. Divide the wall measurement by the stamp measurement to determine the exact wall height that will accommodate a whole number of diamonds.

3. Use a yardstick level and pencil to lightly mark a vertical and horizontal grid on the wall for the patterned area to help with placement of stamps. The grid squares should be the same size as the above stamp measurement.

4. To help with placement of the fleur-de-lis stamps on the upper portion of the wall, extend some of the vertical guidelines up from the lower portion of the wall.

5. Pour a bit of each acrylic paint onto a foam plate. With a small foam brush, apply several colors separately to different parts of the stamp. Allow colors to overlap slightly, but do not blend them together or you will lose the variation in the stamped motif.

6. Turn the stamp at an angle and center it over a section of the wall where the grid lines intersect, aligning each of the four corner points with a line. Visually check the alignment before pressing the stamp to the surface to ensure it will align with the diamonds to follow.

7. Place the stamp against the wall and rock gently to transfer the paint. Reload with paint and repeat process, stamping green diamonds at every other grid intersection.

8. Load fleur-de-lis stamp with paint as above. Stamp randomly, centering the stamp over the grid intersection in selected open spaces between the green squares. Do not fill every open square. Also, randomly stamp the design on the plain wall above the checked treatment, following vertical grid lines.

9. In three separate containers, mix equal amounts of glaze base with each of the following paint colors: bright yellow, butter yellow and pale yellow. Pour a little of each of the yellow-toned glaze colors into separate small paint trays. Randomly pick up one or two of the glazes with one 4" foam roller.

10. To create the yellow diamonds that are centered over the remaining grid intersections, set the 4" roller on the diagonal so it is aligned between the points of two green diamonds and roll out a diamond using the points and the edges of the diagonal rows of tile stamps as guidelines (see photo A). If desired, flip the roller and apply paint in the opposite direction for variation or to add more paint. Skip the areas filled with the fleur-de-lis stamp.

11. Create the cream diamonds that fill in all the open spaces between both the yellow and green stamped diamonds. As above, use a new 4" foam roller and glazes made with three different hues of cream. To add to the aged look and create interest, randomly brush or roll the cream paint slightly into the edges of some green stamped and yellow diamonds (see photo B).

12. Use the foam rollers to randomly apply a mixture of some of the yellow and cream glazes to the upper wall area. Use both rollers at the same time, overlapping the colors to recreate the look of old, painted plaster.

SHOPPING LIST

- Flat latex paint in gold (for the base coat) and 1 quart each of bright yellow, butter yellow, pale yellow and 3 different hues of cream (for mixing glazes)
- Glaze base
- Yardstick level
- Pencil
- Fleur-de-lis and architectural tile rubber stamps
- Small foam paintbrushes
- Acrylic craft paint in forest green, khaki, mint green, pale aqua and pale gray-green
- 4" foam rollers
- Small paint trays

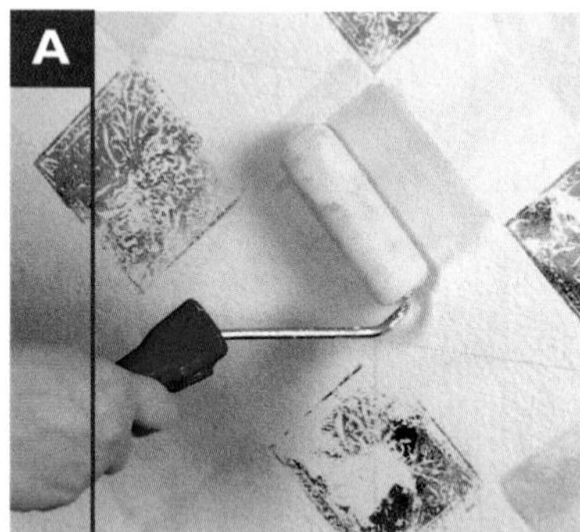

A

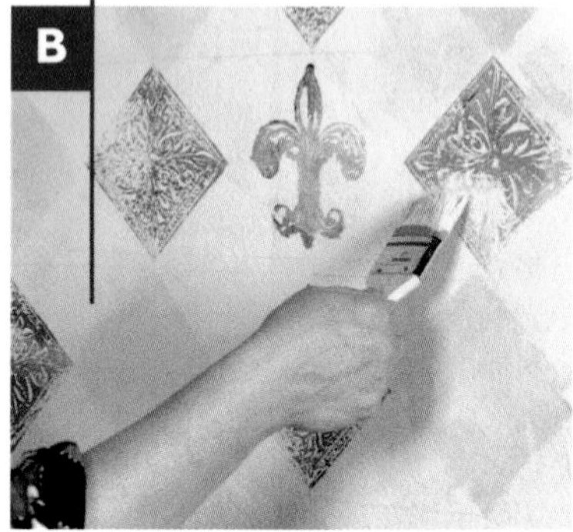

B

INSTANT AGING

TO CREATE THE AGED FRESCO LOOK, you want variation in the stamping. Here's how:

- As you stamp, alter the use of color on the stamp. For example, use all light colors one time and all dark the next or create a mix of the two.
- Apply the paint more heavily in some areas than others. Some of the crevices of the design may fill with paint, but that will only enhance the weathered look.
- Change the quality of the stamping application—sometimes you can use the stamp twice before reloading it with paint, resulting in one darker and one lighter image.

GLINT OF *Riches*

GOLD-LEAFING IN AN ASSORTMENT OF MIXED METALS adds elegant shimmer to the amber tones of a color-washed wall. Apply the leafing by hand to give each stenciled motif a unique combination of colors and textures. Find a stencil design you like or create your own using stencil acetate. Simple shapes are easiest to work with. Our inspiration came from a wall plaque with a fleur-de-lis shape. Colorwash the wall with a combination of gold and tan glazes (see Washed in Color chapter for more on this technique). Determine the placement of the stencils and lightly mark on the wall with pencil. (Our motifs were placed on the wall in a random pattern, with about 24 inches between each repeat.) Apply stencil adhesive to the back of the stencil and press it against the wall in one of the marked locations. With a pencil, trace the stencil outline onto the wall. Remove stencil and continue until all outlines are complete. Using a small artist brush, apply leafing adhesive to the wall within the stencil outline, being sure to cover the pencil outlines. Let the adhesive dry until it is clear. Using your finger, apply multicolored gold leafing flakes to the adhesive, gently patting them in place (see photo). Let dry about 1 hour. Brush off loose flakes using a large artist brush. Repeat process until all motifs are complete. Seal with a clear matte polyacrylic sealer, if desired.

LETTER PERFECT

SIGN IN WITH AN ORNATE STENCILED INITIAL to create a personalized focal point. This commands attention over a furniture piece or fireplace and provides inexpensive wall art. Look for manuscript initials in clip art or in calligraphy books, and enlarge them to fit your wall space. To make a stencil, place acetate over the enlarged letter, trace the design and cut it out with a craft knife. Spray the stencil back with adhesive and apply it to the wall, using a level for placement. Use a makeup sponge to dab paint onto the stencil. For an aged look, vary the amount of paint applied to the wall.

AGELESS

SOMETIMES ONLY NATURE CAN PROVIDE the right tools for an original paint finish, as illustrated by this border stamped with evergreen boughs. Use it at ceiling or chair-rail height or to frame a window or door. Cut three to four small boughs of pine. Place a drop cloth on the floor next to the wall where you'll be loading the greens with paint. Base-coat wall with sage green flat latex paint. Let dry. Place a bough on scrap paper and coat with cream-colored paint using a roller. Lightly press the painted bough against a piece of paper to remove excess paint. Press the bough against the wall, using your opposite hand to press down each needle. Repeat until you have finished your design. Load a cotton swab with light green paint, then twist and lightly drag the tip across the wall from one bunch of needles to another to create a branch effect. For pinecone shapes, use another cotton swab dipped in light green paint. Roll it onto the wall, forming small clusters of irregular shaped dots (see photo). Make the dots smaller as you work out to the tip of the pinecone. Reload the swab with paint or switch to a new swab as needed. Highlight pinecones on one side by adding dots of cream paint with a fresh cotton swab. Fill in sparse areas by stamping with a small bunch of needles loaded with paint. Use an artist brush and paint to fill in areas where transferred image is incomplete or too light.

WE ALL KNOW THE EARTH isn't flat, so why should your walls be? You can give them texture and depth with a variety of paint treatments or take it a step further and actually add dimension with objects and materials. Go the natural route, with bits of straw, dried florals or wood boards, or incorporate man-made items, like wire fencing and plaster me dallions, into your design.

RADISH
FLOWERING KALE

TEXTURED BACKDROP

TO CREATE A TEXTURED WALL SURFACE, mix joint compound with water until it is the consistency of peanut butter. Apply it to the wall using a trowel. Let dry. Add layers of compound until you have desired texture, letting dry between coats. Apply white latex primer to walls to prevent glaze from soaking in. Let dry.

BREAK THE *Mold*

1. Mix one part plum paint with three parts glaze base. Pour the glaze mixture into a paint tray. Working on one small area at a time, use a 1"-nap roller cover to apply the glaze mixture to the wall. (The thick nap helps prevent heavy glaze application.) Apply glaze more heavily in some areas, blending out at the edges to soften.

2. While glaze is still wet, wipe with a rag in a circular motion, removing more glaze in some areas to create interest. Continue process until all walls are complete.

3. For more dimension, make glaze mixtures with blackberry and iris blue paints. Add touches of each randomly on wall as above. Use light, random strokes when brushing on the color. Apply the glaze only in certain areas so plum remains the most prominent color.

4. Determine arrangement of medallions on your wall. (To create a headboard above our twin bed, we evenly spaced 17 large medallions of varying designs in an arch shape, beginning about 6 inches above the mattress. We filled in randomly with smaller medallions and scattered some above the arch.) If creating a headboard design, find and mark center of bed on wall and mark approximate placement of each medallion. To help plan layout, make several photocopies of each medallion and arrange them on the wall or floor.

5. Following manufacturer's instructions, prepare plaster. Pour the plaster slowly and evenly into the molds and tap to bring air bubbles to the surface (see photo A). Let plaster dry until it is firm to the touch, yet damp. Turn the tray over and pop out the molded pieces. Repeat until you have made all the medallions needed for your design. Air dry on paper towels for 24 to 36 hours, depending on the humidity. (To reduce drying time, place on a cookie sheet in an oven on a very low setting.)

6. Brush a coat of latex primer over the medallions. Let dry.

7. Lightly brush a coat of plum glaze onto each medallion (see photo B). (We used only plum glaze; you can use additional colors, if desired.) Wipe off excess glaze with a rag, leaving in the grooves to highlight the design. Let dry.

8. Apply a small amount of caulk to the center back of the center medallion (see photo C). Place the medallion at the marked centerpoint on the wall above the bed and press until it adheres. Apply caulk to the other medallions and position each on the wall in the desired location until design is complete. Let dry at least 24 hours.

SHOPPING LIST

- Flat latex paint in plum
- Glaze base
- Roller paint tray
- Paint roller and 1"-nap roller cover
- Rags
- Acrylic craft paint in iris blue and blackberry
- Paintbrushes
- Plastic molds for candy or soap, in floral, leaf and medallion patterns
- Plaster of Paris
- Latex primer
- Latex window/door caulk
- Caulking gun

A

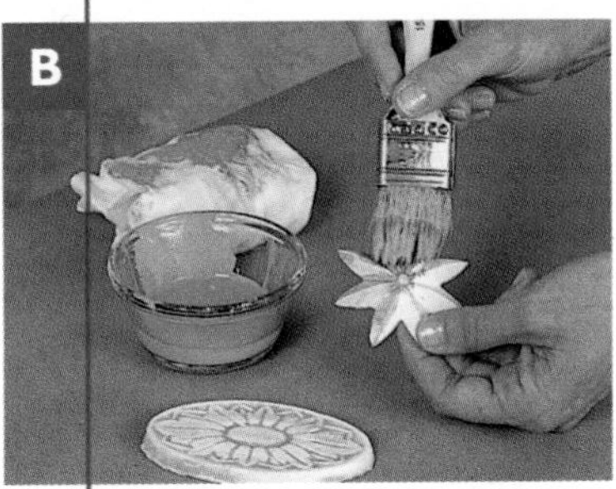
B

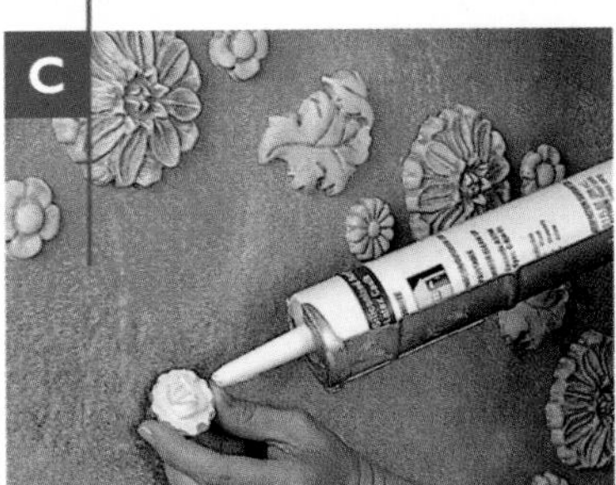
C

LEAF *Collage*

1. Base coat the wall with ivory paint. Let dry. (Even though the overlay paper is very sheer, it may change the color of the base coat. Be sure to test the two together on a practice board.)

2. Select dried leaves and pressed flowers. We chose flowers in natural colors. Some of the leaves we chose were natural, some were dyed and some were skeletonized leaves with little coloration. To add color to the latter, we sprayed them with green, burgundy and terra-cotta hues that coordinate with the other leaf and flower colors. If you'd like to change the color of your leaves, work in a well-ventilated area, lay leaves on a protected surface and lightly spray with desired colors. Let dry.

3. Determine leaf and flower placement on the wall. We randomly placed leaves and flowers, trying to balance color, leaf shape and size across the wall, positioning the leaves and petals to appear as if they had just fallen from a tree.

4. Working on one 2-foot by 2-foot section at a time, coat the surface of the wall with sealer using a 4" foam roller. While the area is still wet, position leaves or flowers on the wall (see photo A).

5. Lay a sheet of tissue paper over the leaves and flowers. Apply sealer over the paper on top of the leaves and flowers using a roller (see photo B). This will seal the items under the paper and dry to an almost transparent finish. Continue to cover the wall with leaves and flowers, overlapping the sheets of paper as you go. We also placed sheets of paper in areas where we did not apply leaves and flowers for continuity in the wall finish. (If the treatment continues onto another wall, bend some leaves around corners and position flowers so they flow from wall to wall.)

6. Step back from the wall often to make sure the distribution of leaves and flowers is balanced. Go back and insert leaves or flowers in those places that need additional coverage, as above.

SHOPPING LIST

- Flat latex paint in ivory
- Sheets of white tissue paper or Japanese paper
- Various dried leaves, pressed flowers and skeletonized craft leaves
- Floral spray paint in burgundy, terra-cotta and two green hues
- Satin-finish sealer
- 4" foam roller

A

B

PRESSING FLOWERS

IF YOU WISH TO USE A COLLECTION OF YOUR OWN FLOWERS and leaves, allow time for pressing and drying. Select naturally flat leaves, flowers or ferns with low-moisture content. Pick your posies on a warm, dry sunny day and snip flowers close to the stems to cut down on moisture, which slows the drying process and speeds decay. Use a flower press following manufacturer's instructions, sandwiching the flowers and leaves between sheets of absorbent paper. (If you don't have a press, another option is to place the flowers and leaves between layers of newspaper and tissue paper inside a book and weigh it down with a brick or heavy rock.) Set aside in a warm, dry area for several weeks.

&GARDEN
TREES
POTTING PLACES

FRENCH *Timber*

PAINTING WALLS

1. Base-coat the wall with yellow paint. Let dry.

2. Mix seven parts clear latex glaze to one part gold paint. Pour mixture into paint tray.

3. Roughly brush out glaze mixture onto a small section of the wall using a paintbrush (see photo A). Work at a fairly quick pace to keep the glaze wet and workable.

4. Using a stippling brush, lightly pounce the tips of the bristles over the glazed section, creating a mottled effect (see photo B). Turn your wrist slightly with each pounce and work in small, odd-shaped patches to keep the pattern random. As you work, use a rag to wipe excess glaze from your brush.

5. Using a badger softening brush, flick the bristles like a feather duster over the glazed surface in all directions to soften and blend the finish, creating a cloudy appearance (see photo C).

Repeat application of glaze in an area adjacent to the last without overlapping onto it. Drag out thinner strokes of glaze when nearing a previously glazed area. Blend the areas together when stippling and softening. Repeat application until wall is covered.

ADDING TIMBERS

1. Make a sketch on graph paper of desired beam placement and estimate spacing, then measure your wall to determine how much lumber will be needed.

2. Distress 1 x 4 boards using a hammer, wire brush or chisel. For a hand-hewn effect, shave down some edges using a utility knife. Lightly sand with medium-grit sandpaper.

3. Stain boards with forest green or another color that complements your furniture and accessories.

4. When boards are dry, lean them up against the wall to determine spacing and create a rough layout. Loosely tack a few boards together using finishing nails to create a chair rail or cross beam to see how the final placement will appear. Mark, measure and number the boards and the wall in the rough layout for easy installation.

5. Remove boards from wall and make any needed cuts using a jigsaw.

6. Install boards on wall with 1½" finishing nails, working from the floor up. For permanent installation, apply construction adhesive to backs of boards before nailing.

7. Wipe a bit of the wall paint and glaze onto the edges of the stained boards to add to the aged look.

WEATHERED WOODS

MIMIC THE EXPOSED BEAMS on the wall of a French farmhouse with distressed 1 x 4 boards. Here, we paired a green stain with warm yellow walls that resemble old plaster. You might try staining the boards gray or brown before distressing them and adding them to walls with a textured paint finish in crisp white or a deep red colorwash, depending on the mood you wish to create.

SHOPPING LIST

- Satin latex paint in yellow and gold
- Interior wood stain in forest green
- Glaze base
- 3" paintbrush
- Badger softening brush
- Stippling brush
- 1 x 4 pine boards in 8' or 10' lengths, depending on ceiling height
- Medium-grit sandpaper
- Jigsaw
- 1½" finishing nails
- Paint tray
- Graph paper
- Measuring tape
- Hammer, wire brush or chisel
- Utility knife (optional)

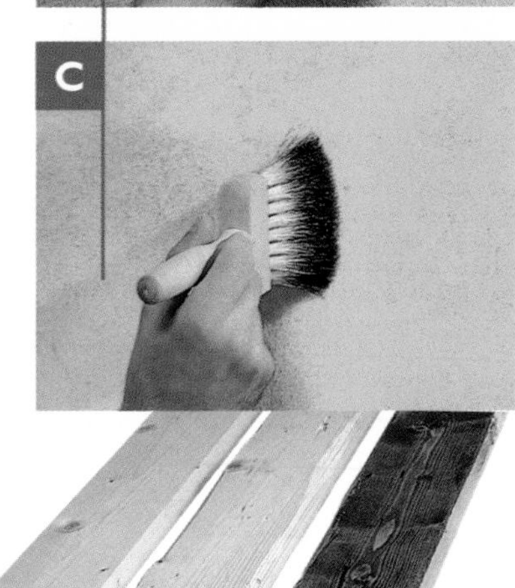

TRICK Brick

IF YOU LIKE EXPOSED BRICK WALLS, but you're surrounded by drywall, don't despair—you can get the same look using faux bricks made from foamboard. Begin by priming your walls, then determine the brick size and number of bricks needed to cover your wall. Our bricks are 2½ inches by 7½ inches. Allowing for ¼ inch between bricks, you will need about six bricks per square foot of wall space. Mark off bricks on sheets of 3/16"-thick foamboard. Cut sheets down to manageable size along markings. Use a ruler and utility knife or jigsaw to cut out bricks. If you're using a jigsaw, set up a cutting jig by clamping a scrap board to your work surface. The board acts as a guide to help you cut straight. To ensure evenly spaced bricks, cut out ¼-inch spacers from scrap foamboard. Make a long horizontal one and a shorter vertical one. Draw level lines on wall about every third row for guidelines. Use a caulk gun to apply construction adhesive to the backs of the bricks in a zigzag bead. Do not apply more than a ¼-inch-thick bead. (Make sure you have proper ventilation for this.) Starting in a corner at the bottom of the wall, press bricks in place, using spacers. Slide spacers along the wall as you go. Every other row, start with a half brick so bricks are staggered from row to row. Once adhesive is dry, apply a coat of primer to the surface. Let that dry, then apply a thin layer of joint compound using a plastic trowel. Drag the trowel and pick it up as you go to add crevices and bumps. Build up layers as desired. Using your fingers or a rag, remove some of the compound from the joints to create the appearance of mortar. Paint the surface tan, using a long-nap roller, and let dry. Finish by dry-rolling white primer on top for a weathered look.

SHEERLY PRETTY

FOR A QUICK AND INEXPENSIVE WAY TO DRESS UP WALLS, try draping them with fabric. Sheer panels are especially pretty against a deeply colored backdrop. It's a great way to hide ugly walls or perk up tired ones, and the treatment is easily removed when you're ready for something new. This treatment features tab-top sheers hung from wall-mounted curtain wire. Measure the width of your walls to determine the amount of curtain wire and size/amount of curtain panels needed. Mount curtain wire at a height that allows the curtain panels to hang just above the floor, using fitting provided and following manufacturer's instructions. Thread the curtain wire through the tabs in the top of panels. Adjust curtain tabs, covering the wall fittings with the end tabs, if desired. If you like, wrap the curtain wire with ribbon or strips of fabric to give it a soft edge.

FENCED In

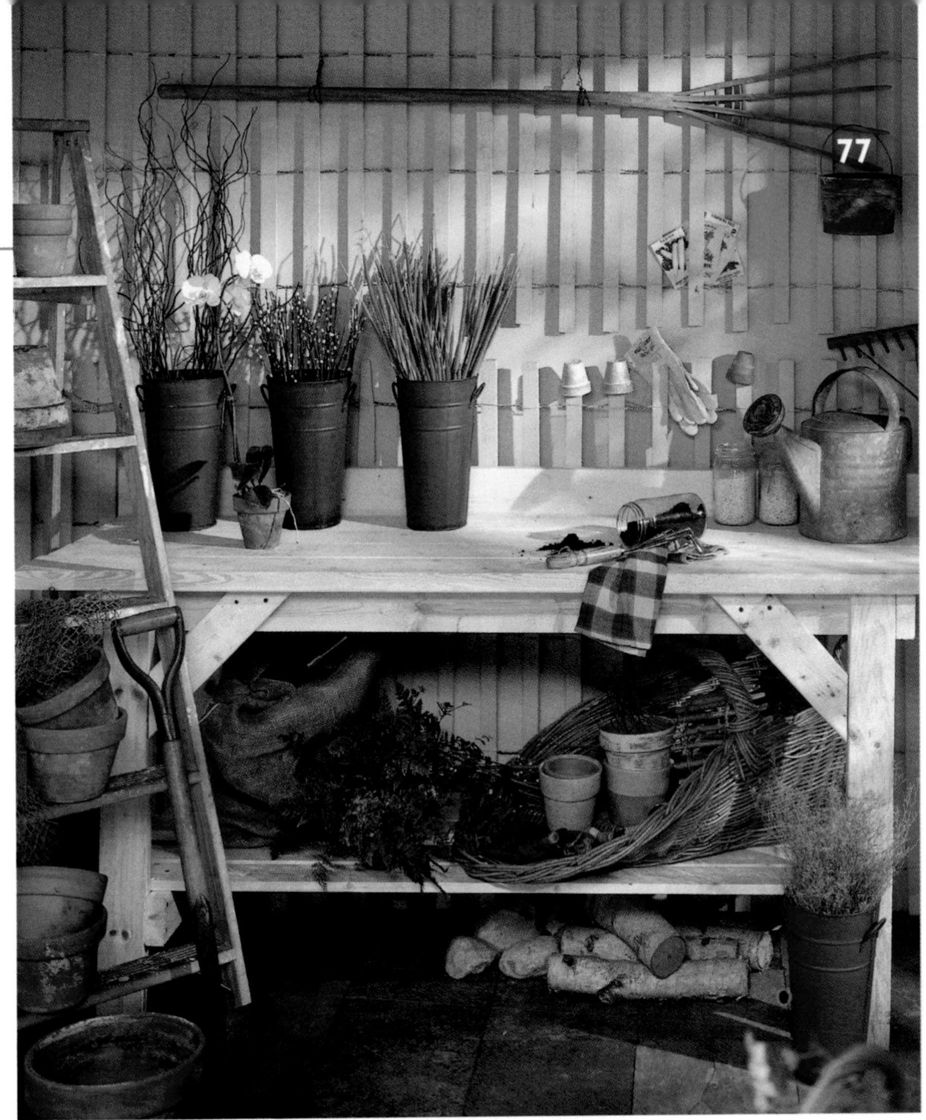

PERFECT FOR A WORKSHOP OR CRAFT ROOM, utility fencing is a primitive country alternative to pegboard—attach it to your wall with screws and use S hooks for hanging items. For a different look, you could install the fencing in vertical rows or apply it only up to chair-rail height. Base-coat wall with desired color (we used a celery hue). Use tin snips to cut two lengths of wood-and-wire utility fencing (it usually comes in 4' x 50' rolls) to fit the length of your wall. (To cover the height of a standard 8-foot wall, we installed two horizontal rows of fencing.) Fasten fencing to the wall using a drill and 1½" wood screws. Trim any extra wire from the end sections. Roll the base color over the fencing using a short-nap roller. (If you'd like to accentuate the fencing, paint it a different color than the base coat before installation.)

PLASTER AND STRAW

ROUGH PLASTER WITH EMBEDDED BITS OF STRAW evokes the thick walls of a rural Provençal farmhouse. Mix joint compound with water to the consistency of peanut butter. Apply it to the wall with a trowel, working in approximately 3-foot by 3-foot sections. Using a sweeping motion, build up the thickness of the drywall compound until it will support pieces of straw. While the drywall compound is wet, place pieces of craft straw (sold in bags at crafts stores) on the wall. Press along the full length of the piece until it adheres to the wall (see photo). Arrange the straw in a random manner, changing the direction of pieces and varying the length of the straw as it is applied. Some portions of the straw may not completely adhere to the wall. In these areas, use a trowel to apply more compound, especially over the ends of the straw. (In some cases, part of the straw will protrude even though the piece is adequately adhered to the wall. This creates interest.) Complete the rest of the wall and let dry. Mix one part straw-colored flat latex paint to three parts glaze. Pour the glaze mixture into a paint tray. Again working in 3-foot by 3-foot sections, use a roller with a 1"-nap sleeve to apply the mixture to random areas of the textured wall surface. Vary the amount of glaze across the wall and allow some plain drywall compound to peek through for an interesting color balance. Use a foam brush to further spread and blend the glaze randomly onto the wall. Continue until the wall is complete. After the paint has dried, apply a coat of matte non-yellowing acrylic sealer using a roller.

80

POWERFUL *Pattern*

82

PATTERN CAN PERK UP A WALL like nothing else. Whether you're mad for plaid or hip to be square, pattern can add a subtle sense of style or make a bold statement, depending on the scale, colors and motifs you choose. Make it precise, using tape or stencils to fashion your designs, or go with the flow to create more random effects inspired by tools and materials, from brushes to bubble wrap.

84

86

WINDOWPANE *Check*

1. Base-coat the wall with white paint. (The base color should be lighter than and compatible with the colors you use to make the plaid stripes in order to achieve a translucent feel.)

2. Measure the length and width of the area to be covered. Sketch out your plaid pattern (we used a windowpane check) on paper. Transfer the plaid pattern to your wall, making adjustments, if necessary. Start at the center of the wall so the pattern works out evenly at each corner. Using a yardstick level and colored pencils similar to the stripe colors, measure and mark the plaid pattern on the wall (see photo A). Begin measuring and marking all the vertical lines, then measure and mark all the horizontal lines.

3. Mix each paint color with glaze, using nine parts glaze and one part paint. (The colors should be semi-transparent. When two colors overlap, the bottom color should be visible through the top color, so it is important that the colors coordinate well.)

4. Following the pencil guidelines, use a 1" foam brush with country blue to paint the medium stripes, centering the brush between the appropriate pencil marks. Paint both the vertical and horizontal stripes. Let dry between coats.

5. Following the guidelines as above, use a 2" foam brush with blue-green paint (see photo B) to paint the large vertical and horizontal stripes. Let paint dry between coats.

6. Following the guidelines as above, use a ½" paintbrush with yellow-green paint to paint the small vertical and horizontal stripes (see photo C). Let paint dry between coats.

SHOPPING LIST

- Flat latex paint in white, country blue, blue-green and yellow-green
- Colored pencils to match paint colors
- Paper
- Glaze base
- Yardstick level
- 1" and 2" foam brushes
- ½" paintbrush

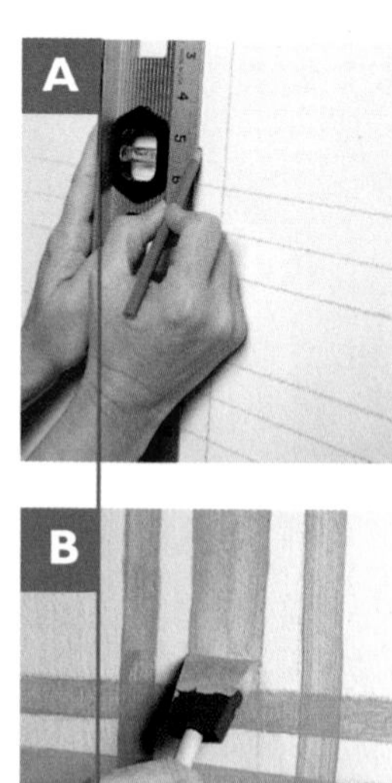

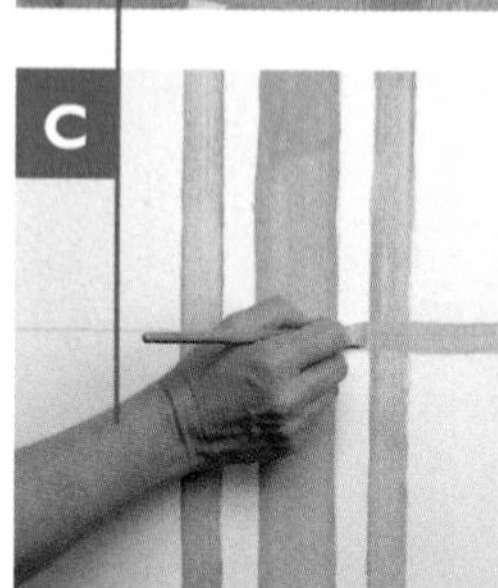

MAD FOR PLAID?

A PATTERN BORROWED from a favorite tea towel or ceramic vase looks crisp and cheerful when recreated larger than life on your kitchen or dining room walls. For this pattern, we measured and marked the wall carefully, then used three widths of paintbrushes to fashion the stripes. If you want to create a more solid plaid pattern, either on a full wall or just up to chair-rail height, you can use different widths of painters tape to mask off intersecting vertical and horizontal stripes. Pick two or three colors to use atop a neutral base coat, and mix each one with glaze base (about one part paint to two parts glaze). The glaze gives the colors translucency so you can apply sheer, overlapping layers. Tape off and apply glaze to your horizontal striping first, using one color at a time, then move on to the vertical stripes to achieve the plaid effect.

TWISTS & *Turns*

SHOPPING LIST

- Ruler/level
- Scissors or utility knife
- Flat latex paint in yellow, orange, burnt orange, brick red and tan
- Glaze base
- Shaper tool with firm angle chisel tip
- Baby wipes or paper towels
- Painters tape
- Foam brushes

1. Create a grid for the base coat. This serves a dual purpose: It is a guide for the topcoat and it helps create a repetitive design. Measure your wall to determine what size squares or rectangles are needed for your wall size and pattern. For our wall, we used a grid of 12-inch squares.

2. Use a level and pencil to lightly mark wall with a grid as determined above.

3. For the base coat, determine how your colors should be distributed. We painted every other square a solid color and the remaining squares a random pattern of several colors. Alternate colors from square to square so the mix of color is balanced, drawing your eye across the wall. With pencil, make a mark on the squares to be painted a solid color.

4. Tape off the marked squares. At the points where the corners of neighboring squares meet, use a straightedge and scissors or a utility knife (using very light pressure—just enough to cut through the tape) to trim the excess tape away, revealing the points. Paint the taped-off squares in solid colors. Remove tape and let paint dry.

5. Tape off squares to be painted with random patterns. Paint these squares with various patterns to create a patchwork effect (see photo A). Work with one color at a time. For example, apply bright yellow in desired squares, let paint dry, then move on to the next color. Continue until you use all of the colors. Vary the distribution of color, using two colors in some squares and three or four colors in others. Step back and check color composition as you work, making sure colors are distributed evenly. Let paint dry.

6. Mix two parts tan paint with one part glaze. (Make sure there is enough glaze to extend drying time but not so much that the mixture becomes too translucent.)

7. Starting at a top corner of the wall, use a foam brush to paint an even coat of glaze mixture over one colored square. Work on one square at a time to ensure ample working time before paint dries. Allow the glaze to set for 10 seconds to 1 minute. If you wait too long, the topcoat will dry and the colors on the base coat will not show through.

8. With the shaper tool, create your design in the topcoated square (see photo B). We used a squiggle pattern, but straight lines or curves would work as well. Practice on a scrap board to get a feel for using the tool. Because the tool lifts off the paint, it may get messy. Keep a paper towel or baby wipe on hand to wipe off excess paint and clean up pattern lines if paint smears. (If you make a mistake, quickly paint over it with the glaze mixture or touch up later when the paint has dried.)

9. Move on to the next square and repeat the process until the entire wall is complete.

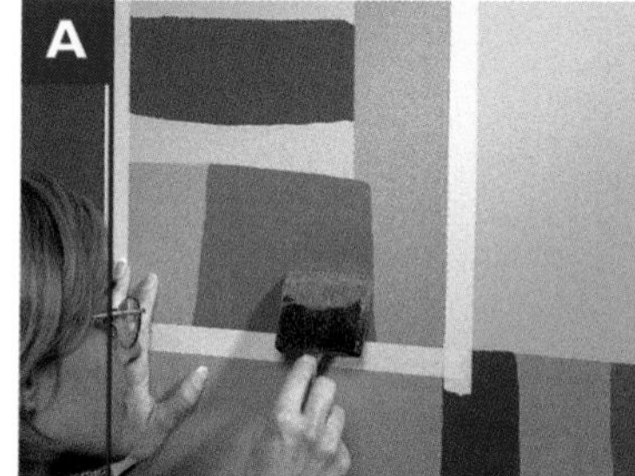
A

B

PREST-O CHANGE-O

THIS TECHNIQUE is similar to the "magic" paint boards seen on television, where you manipulate the top layer of paint to reveal a multicolored pattern underneath. This works for many color combinations. Visit your local paint store and experiment with color chips to see what works well together. Consider how paints of different finishes and colors would affect this treatment. Also, you could choose to paint the entire wall with random patterns instead of alternating with solid squares to produce a different finished look.

BLENDED *Blocks*

1. Base-coat the wall with white paint. Let dry.

2. At the paint store, have glazes of each color mixed, using one part glazing medium and one part paint. (A quart (half paint and half glaze) of each mixture should be enough for a 10-foot by 10-foot room because there are so many colors and the glaze is applied very lightly.)

3. Use a yardstick level and pencil to lightly mark the wall with a grid of 8-inch squares.

4. Plan color placement. Start with the color that you want to emphasize the most. Space the color evenly but randomly over the surface of the wall, trying not to repeat the same color in nearby rows or squares. For precision, draw a small plan of your wall before starting, coloring in the squares to determine the desired pattern. Our walls were 8-foot by 8-foot, so 144 squares fit on each wall. We repeated each color at least 15 times on a wall and then used the leftover squares to repeat a few of the colors, in this case the lighter greens and yellows. A few squares were left unpainted, except where color from the surrounding squares was brushed onto them.

5. Start with one color of glaze, filling the chosen squares. Pour that glaze onto a foam plate and apply to the wall with a chip brush. As you apply the color to each square, brush some of it vertically and horizontally, extending it beyond the edges into the neighboring squares (see photo A), creating a blend of colors. Use random brush strokes of varying size.

6. Lightly drag a rag vertically and horizontally across the square to lift off excess glaze and create random streaks for added textural interest.

7. Continue adding colors, one at a time, until all of the colors have been used. Go back and fill in the remaining squares with hues that best highlight your color scheme. As you work, step back frequently to evaluate color placement.

8. After filling in all of the squares, look at the wall from a distance to decide where to brush on more glaze to lighten or darken areas and ensure a balance of color.

SHOPPING LIST

- Flat latex paint in white
- 1 quart each of latex paint mixed with glaze in poppy, dark tan, brass, green bean, loden green, clover green, ocean blue and light spinach green
- Glaze base
- Yardstick level
- 3" chip brushes (one for each color)
- Rags
- Foam plates

A

COLOR ALTERNATIVES

IF YOU LIKE THE LOOK of this softly blended checkerboard-style treatment, but want to use other colors, such as pastels or brights, that coordinate with your furnishings and fabrics, just choose analogous colors that are all close in value. For example, use colors that are all midtones. Experiment to find the combination you like best. Steer clear of pairing complementary colors; when blended together, they will produce a muddy effect.

THE WOVEN VERTICAL AND HORIZONTAL STRIPES OF GINGHAM FABRIC easily translate to walls using glaze applied with a roller. Tape off your trim and ceiling. Paint the wall with vanilla-colored paint. Then, measure the wall length and height to determine the best width and spacing of the vertical and horizontal stripes. (To fit your wall dimensions, you may need to make adjustments in spacing. You can do this at the corners and ceiling where it will be less noticeable.) We used 4-inch-wide vertical and horizontal stripes, spaced 4 inches apart, to create a gingham pattern. Rather than masking off stripes, we marked our guidelines 8 inches apart on the wall. To paint the stripes, we followed along each guideline, always placing the 4" roller on the same side. This method produces softer, fabric-like edges. Using a yardstick level and a colored pencil, measure and mark guidelines on the wall. (Choose a pencil a few shades lighter than your paint color so the lines will be hidden after painting.) Find the center of the wall and begin to measure and mark vertical guidelines 8 inches apart, extending from the top of the wall to the floor. Work from the center outward, leaving approximately 2 inches at the corners. Mark horizontal guidelines 8 inches apart, beginning at the midline and working out until you reach the floor and ceiling. Mix one part paint (we used sky blue) with two parts glaze. Using a 4" roller, apply the mixture following the vertical guidelines. Paint following the horizontal guidelines in the same manner, overlapping the vertical stripes to complete the design. Sand following the directions of the stripes with fine-grit sandpaper to soften the edges and reveal some of the base coat.

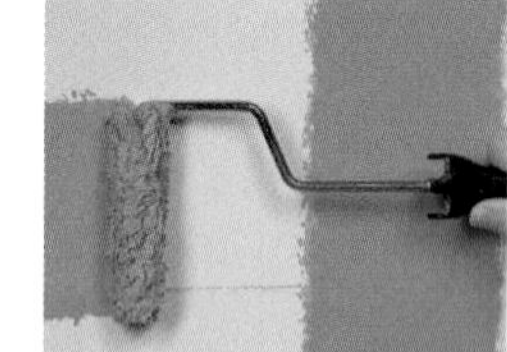

GOOD-NATURED *Gingham*

THE GRASS IS ALWAYS GREENER

FOR WALLS THAT MIMIC A GRASSY MEADOW, try this treatment that calls for altering a plain paintbrush. Begin by base-coating the wall with a light green paint in a satin finish. Cut the bristles out of a 2" chip brush to form irregular notches. You may use a larger brush, but the 2" size will produce wispier strokes. Mix one part blue-green satin-finish latex paint with two parts glaze. Use the altered brush to make strokes about a foot long, curving off to both sides at the end of the stroke to mimic the appearance of grass. For some strokes, start at the top and brush down. For others, start at the base and brush upward. Use a light pressure so the blades of grass appear distinct. Work in small irregular sections approximately 3 feet by 3 feet, overlapping grasses slightly as you work across the wall. To lighten up any dark areas, dry brush over them using another notched chip brush and white paint.

A BIT *Bubbly*

THIS TREATMENT PUTS BUBBLE WRAP TO WORK in a novel way—creating cheerful stripes. Base-coat wall in flat tan paint. Let dry overnight. Plan the size and placement of your stripes. Adjust the sizes of stripes to fit your room. Start measuring for your stripes from each wall's centerline and plan sizes so the stripes work out evenly. If needed, make adjustments at the room's corners. (We created 6-inch bubble-wrap imprinted stripes spaced about 12 inches apart). Measure and mark stripe placement on walls with yardstick level and pencil, then mask off the stripes with painters tape. Mix one part bright coral latex paint with two to three parts glaze base. Beginning at the ceiling, brush a thin coat of the glaze mixture halfway down a stripe using a foam paintbrush. (If you work on a larger section, the glaze may dry before you have time to apply the bubble wrap.) While glaze is still wet, carefully place bubble wrap onto the wall and press firmly. Use large-size bubble wrap in about 7-inch by 24-inch strips. You can use each strip a few times, wiping clean between uses. Make sure you have extras in case some strips become damaged or paint-clogged. Peel the bubble wrap off the wall (see photo). Apply the glaze to the lower half of the strip, blending with a foam paintbrush to eliminate paint lines between sections. Complete remaining stripes as above, then remove tape and let dry.

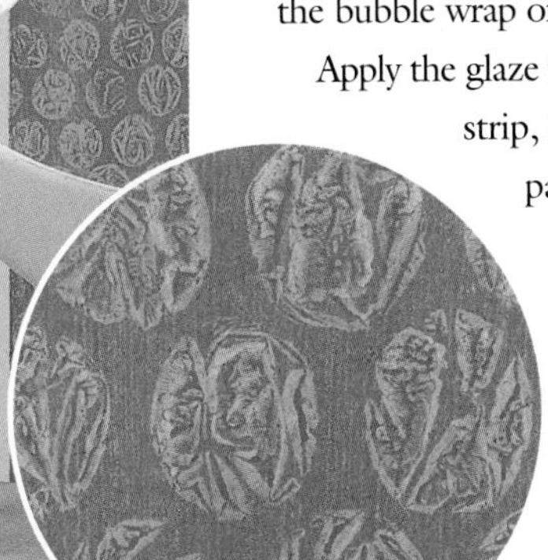

PAPER *Pairings*

92

WALLS AND PAPER GO WAY BACK—since the 1400s, wallpaper has been an easy and economical way to dress up an interior. Even if you're turned off by sticky paste and pattern matching, you might find that it's fun to add a touch of paper to your walls, using such diverse sources as newspaper, decorative tissue, scrapbook-paper cutouts and photocopied letters. And, you can even fix past mistakes or quickly update a room by painting over old wallpaper.

Colors

DRY BRUSHED *Wallpaper*

1. Choose three similar paint colors for the main paint treatment—a midtone for the base coat, a darker color for the second layer and a lighter color for the topcoat—and a fourth accent color that coordinates with your wallpaper. For simplicity, choose colors from the same paint strip. Or, select paint colors with different undertones (e.g., pink with a blue cast, such as mauve, as opposed to pink with a yellow cast that leans toward peach) to will make the wall more visually interesting.

2. With a chip brush, paint around and isolate selected wallpaper motifs with the midtone base-coat color (see photo A). Paint up to about ¼" from the edges of each motif to create a general outline; do not try to follow the details of each shape exactly. Let dry. (As you work, do not load the brush too heavily. Saturating the paper may loosen the adhesive and cause bubbling.)

3. Fill in the background areas with the base-coat paint. For an even lighter look, paint over entire motifs or portions of motifs. Let dry.

4. Dry brush the remaining colors over the base coat, using a lighter application for each layer. Pour a little of the darker second color onto a foam plate. Dip the tips of a 2" or 3" chip brush into the paint and wipe excess on a paper towel. Dry brush paint around the motifs, allowing some base coat to remain visible (see photo B). Let dry. Apply a second coat for thicker texture. Paint mainly in the center of the base-coated areas, blending in toward the motifs. Leave some base-coated areas completely untouched. Sweep the brush lightly over the wallpaper motifs to soften printed images. Let dry.

5. Pour the accent color onto a foam plate. Dry brush over the previous layers, barely sweeping the brush tips over the surface. (Because paint is applied thickly using a coarse-bristled brush, previous brush strokes leave ridges that capture the succeeding layer of paint.) Colors should begin to soften and blend. For variety, blend this color over some areas where only the base coat shows. As you work, step back to examine the wall, making sure color distribution is balanced. If needed, go back and dry brush some of the previous colors to further soften and blend edges.

6. Add topcoat color over previous layers, dry brushing evenly over all painted areas and sweeping the brush lightly in various directions over exposed wallpaper motifs (see photo C). Blend painted surfaces with wallpaper by using a brush to lightly rub paint randomly around the motif edges.

SHOPPING LIST

- Flat latex paint in four colors that coordinate with wallpaper (we used medium peach, light peach, coral and terra-cotta)
- Painters tape
- 2" or 3" chip brushes, one for each color
- Paper towels
- Foam plates

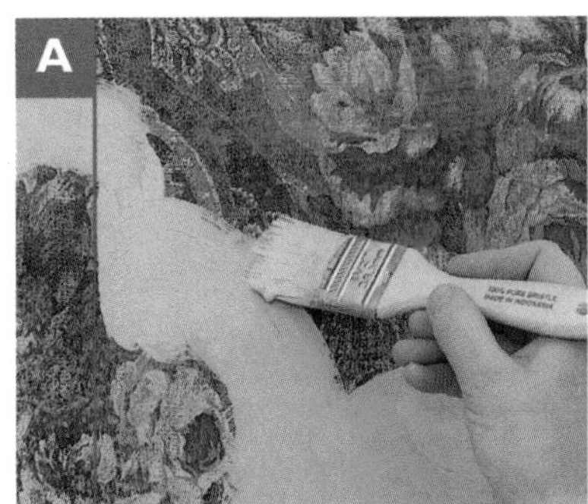
A

B

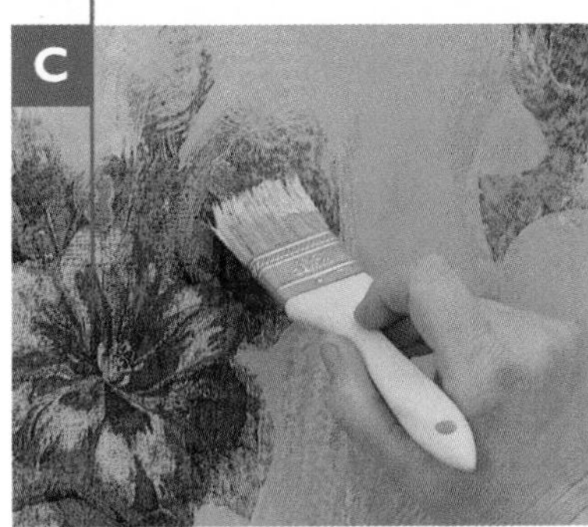
C

PLAIN WALLS? NO PROBLEM!

THIS IS A GREAT WAY TO CHANGE THE LOOK of old wallpaper, but if your walls are not already papered, you can achieve a similar effect by cutting floral motifs from a roll or two of wallpaper. Plan and mark flower placement on the wall so that motifs are evenly distributed, use wallpaper paste to adhere the cutouts at the marked points, then proceed with the paint technique.

LARGER-THAN-LIFE *Letters*

1. Make enlarged copies of the letter and envelope using an oversize copier at a printing shop. We enlarged our original letter and envelope 200 percent and then continued to enlarge them from there until they were the desired size. Make copies in several different sizes to add variation and visual interest to the finished treatment.

2. Wrinkle some of the copies in selected areas. When you later apply paint to antique the paper, it will gather in the folds, making the paper look even older.

3. Dampen the copies by misting them with a spray bottle filled with water.

4. Thin the tan acrylic paint slightly with water. Apply thinned paint randomly to the paper using a sea sponge (see photo A). Repeat the process with brown acrylic paint for an aged effect. Blot off excess with sponge.

5. Again wrinkle some of the pieces. Unfold and let dry.

6. Tear or cut the pieces into irregular shapes of various sizes.

7. Apply a coat of wallpaper primer to the wall. Let dry.

8. Brush wallpaper adhesive onto a section of the wall surface. Adhere the pieces to the wall, one section at a time, as if you were assembling a collage (see photo B). Smooth with wallpaper brush. Repeat until entire wall is covered. (We covered the entire wall; this treatment would look nice just above chair-rail height as well.)

SHOPPING LIST

- Handwritten letter and envelope
- Spray bottle with water
- Acrylic craft paint in shades of brown and tan
- Paintbrush
- Large sea sponge
- Wallpaper primer
- Wallpaper adhesive
- Wallpaper brush

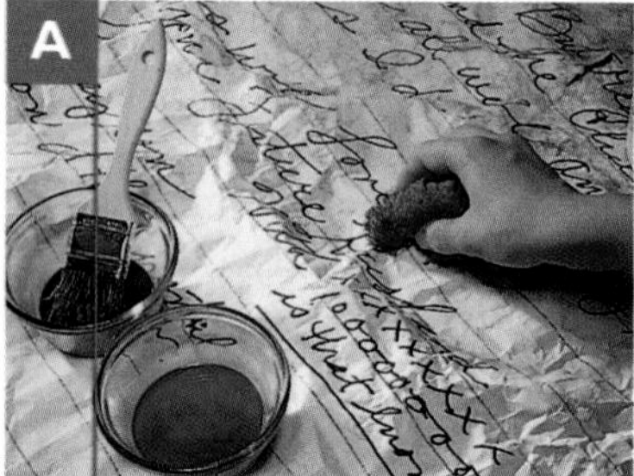
A

B

MORE WAYS WITH WORDS

OUR NOSTALGIC WALL TREATMENT was inspired by the discovery of a 1913 love letter, but other forms of written expression can become the basis of a personalized wall treatment:

- If you don't have letters you'd like to use, try copying a few lines of your favorite poetry, quotations, song lyrics or book passages into longhand and enlarging those for use on the wall.
- For a child's bedroom or playroom, make copies of his or her artwork, writings or cute sayings to cover the walls.
- Cook up a memorable kitchen border using photocopies of grandma's recipe cards.
- Make a scrapbook-like border using black and white copies of favorite family photographs, complete with handwritten captions.

TIP: *To round out the look, make coordinating accessories—decoupage copies of letters onto a headboard, lamp shade, tray or keepsake box. You can even have the image of your letter made into a transfer to embellish a pillow or other fabric item.*

CLEVELAND OHIO
APR 10
3 30 PM
1913
Chicago Ill
74485

PRETTY *Posies*

1. Measure and mark the wall for chair-rail placement, using a yardstick level and pencil. Run a strip of painters tape under the marked line. Paint the upper section of the wall with light lime green paint and the lower section with light aqua paint. Remove tape. Let paint dry.

2. Cut lengths of chair-rail trim to fit your wall and paint white. Let dry. Attach the trim with brads following your paint line.

3. Select scrapbook papers. Arrange the papers on a flat surface or tape them to the wall to plan a balanced layout of color and pattern.

4. Create pot and vase patterns in a variety of sizes and shapes and trace them onto scrapbook papers. Cut out the shapes.

5. Tape cutouts on the wall. Vary the shapes and sizes of the containers and paper designs that will be next to each other. Mark placement of each cutout and each container opening with pencil (see photo A) on the wall. (Indicating container openings will help place flowers.) Remove cutouts, numbering the backs to ensure proper placement when pasting them to the wall.

6. Create flower patterns to fit in containers, drawing simple blooms, like daisies and tulips, with leaves and stems. Determine which floral patterns will go with each container. Transfer floral images onto wall using transfer paper and pencil, following the pots' opening guidelines.

7. Use light leaf green and artist brushes to paint stems and leaves. Use spring green or dark leaf green to paint shadows on the leaves and stems. Thin paints slightly with water for a more transparent look.

8. Use various colors of thinned acrylic paints to create circular flower centers. While wet, highlight by blending in white. Shade white flower centers by brushing a bit of the planned petal color around the perimeters. Add swirls of contrasting color to some flower centers.

9. Use various colors of thinned acrylic paint to create outlines of flower petals and then fill them fill in (see photo B). Add swirls of color and shadows to petals while the paint is still wet. Let dry.

10. Use a foam brush to apply a thin, even coat of wallpaper paste to the backs of the pot and vase cutouts. Align cutouts with the pencil markings on the wall (see photo C). Use a wallpaper brush or scraper to smooth the paper in place and press out excess paste. Wipe surface with damp sponge. Continue to apply the remainder of the pots and vases to the wall.

MIX IT UP

INSTEAD OF CUTTING THE VASES from scrapbook paper, cut out the flower petals, centers and leaves, using paint to make the stems. For the containers, cut pot and vase stencils from acetate and stencil the shapes on the wall, adding handpainted shadows and highlights.

SHOPPING LIST

- Yardstick level
- Pencil
- Painters tape
- Flat latex paint in light lime green, light aqua and white
- Paint tray, roller and roller covers
- Decorative trim for chair rail
- Scrapbook paper in a variety of colors and patterns
- Scissors or craft knife
- Transfer paper
- Round and flat artist brushes
- Acrylic craft paint in light leaf green, spring green, dark leaf green, yellow, pumpkin, red-orange, fuchsia, white and azure blue
- Wallpaper paste
- Brads
- Foam brush
- Wallpaper brush or plastic pan scraper
- Sponge

A

B

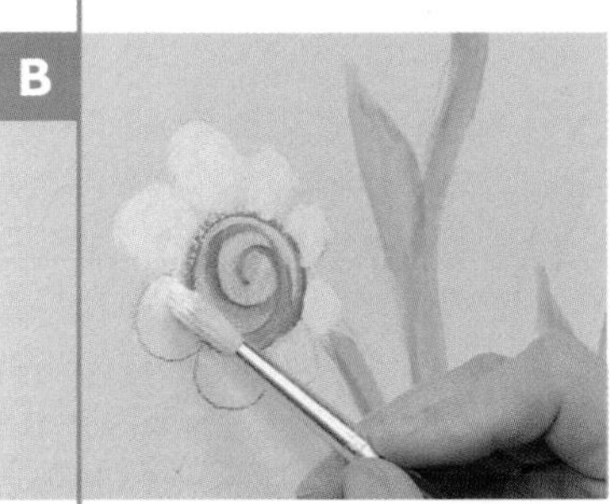

C

DAISY *Cutouts*

GET THE LOOK OF WALLPAPER WITHOUT THE FUSS — no pattern matching or struggling with large sheets of sticky paper. Die-cut shapes are available at stationery or hobby and craft shops in many patterns, colors, shapes and sizes. Choose one that suits your room. Paint walls to coordinate with chosen die-cuts and let dry. Determine the placement of your die-cuts. Use them as an overall wall treatment, as we did, or create a border by lining them up in a row. Measure and mark walls accordingly. We wanted our walls to have a balanced, yet freeform, design, so we arranged flowers of the same size evenly spaced in horizontal rows and staggered the rows vertically to create the look of random placement. Prepare wallpaper paste according to manufacturer's instructions and brush an even coat onto the backs of the die-cuts. Carefully place the shapes on the wall at marked points and smooth out bubbles and excess paste with a plastic pan scraper (see photo). Wipe away excess paste with a rag or moist towel. Continue until the walls are complete.

FRAMED PANELS

CREATE A QUICK-AND-EASY FOCAL POINT using framed wallpaper. Here, we used a red and cream toile to coordinate with the fabrics in our room. This is a great use for wallpaper remnants, and it's temporary—when you're ready for a change, simply replace it with a new pattern without any scraping or steaming. Select three large picture frames, them cut pieces of foam-core board to fit within each frame. Cut wallpaper pieces about 2 inches larger all around than the foamboard. Adhere the wallpaper to the foam-board pieces by applying decoupage medium to back of the paper. Press out any bubbles with a plastic pan scraper. Insert the panels into the frames and hang equally spaced on the wall.

IN THE *News*

THIS TREATMENT IS BEST IN A ROOM with low moisture; we used it in a powder room. Tear newspaper into irregular pieces. Determine placement of pieces on the wall in a random, yet balanced, manner. Prepare cellulose wallpaper paste following manufacturer's instructions. Apply paste to the back of the newspaper pieces with a paintbrush. (Paste may cause the newspaper to yellow upon application, but any paper that is not acid-free will yellow over time. If you wish to prevent this from occurring so rapidly, make photocopies of newspaper, tearing and pasting as above.) Places pieces on wall in desired locations and smooth over them with a 10" plastic taping knife to press out excess paste. Seal all newspaper pieces with matte-finish sealer. Mix drywall compound with water until it is the consistency of peanut butter. Apply the mixture to the wall with a trowel, covering the outer edges of the newspaper pieces, then working outward to cover the remainder of the wall (see photo). Work on one small area at a time. Vary the thickness of compound so it's heavy in some areas and light in others. Let dry overnight. Mix 10 parts previously prepared drywall compound and one part parchment-colored latex paint. Apply a layer of this mixture, allowing some of the previous layer to show through, and let dry. Add a bit more paint to the mixture to darken it, then apply a third layer of color, as above.

RED TISSUE PAPER

SIMPLY SANDWICHING TISSUE PAPER between layers of paint makes this textured treatment easy. Start with a neutral-color base coat. Tear and crumple sheets of tissue paper, creating three types of pieces and sorting them into piles. Make some with two torn edges and a straight edge for along the ceiling and baseboards, some with one torn edge and two straight ones for ceiling and baseboards at the corners, and some with all edges torn for the remainder of the wall. Tape off the ceiling and trim, and then pour poppy red (or your color of choice) satin-finish paint in a tray. Pick up some paint with a large roller and roll onto the wall in a 2-inch by 3-inch wall section. While the paint is still wet, open a sheet of tissue, smooth it slightly and pat it onto the wall. This treatment works well with a two-person team—one to apply paint and the other to smooth out the tissue sheets and hand them to the painter. Next, roll more paint over the top of the tissue paper to secure it to the wall. Continue to apply tissue, overlapping the pieces. If the paint dries before you are done with a section, re-wet the area with paint so the tissue paper will adhere. Repeat until the walls are covered.

MURALS & More

FOR CENTURIES, artists have been using walls as canvases to create large-scale works. Though it may appear daunting, you needn't be a professional or even an accomplished painter to bring a mural to life in your own home. Tricks like using a projector to transfer images to the wall or a grid system to build a picture piece by piece take some of the mystique out of mural painting. If you don't want to attempt a whole wall, start smaller with some oversize artwork, like a single scene or furniture-framing design.

NOT JUST FOR KIDS

PAINT-BY-NUMBER KITS rose to popularity in the 1950s, enabling artists of all ages to create mass-produced masterpieces. They're enjoying a revival today, and you can easily expand on the premise using a projector to transfer the image from a kit onto a wall. Just fill in the squares following the palette or change the palette to coordinate with your room. We started with a fall forest scene in hues of orange, yellow and brown but assigned it new colors of blue, lavender and aqua.

MURAL BY *Number*

1. If you wish to alter the palette of your artwork to fit your decorating scheme, scan the colored artwork on the cover of the package into your computer. Import the image into Photoshop and alter the color by making adjustments using the hue and saturation controls. When satisfied with the color, print out a copy of the picture with the revised color scheme. Use the printout as your color guide for picking new colors. (If you do not have a computer and/or scanner at home, visit your local copy shop for assistance.) You can also use a paint deck or chart to pick a range of analogous colors, selecting those with the same values as the original painting colors in order to maintain the range of light and dark in the painting. Make photocopies of the printed canvas and experiment with colors. Another option is to add white or black to the original colors to create a pastel or darker palette.

2. Choose acrylic paints to match the colors of your printout and make a list of the numbers that correspond to each color. Start with the areas that have a dominant color and coordinate that color with the number on the paint board. If the original palette for your kit contains many areas to be painted a mixture of two colors, you may need to adjust your color choices or pick a premixed paint color and assign it the mix number. For example, in our palette, color 14 was a gray used as the main tree trunk color and color 46 was a blue seen in the leaves. Some shadow areas were marked as 14/46. When these colors were mixed, the result did not match the color printout, so we picked another blue-gray to use.

3. If you are unsure of your color choices, test them by painting a photocopy of the numbered board included in the paint-by-number kit. Make changes to your palette, if desired.

4. To save time when painting, select the most-used color in the artwork as your base coat. We used a light medium blue for our base coat. Base-coat the wall. Let dry.

5. Place a clean photocopy into an image projector. (This works as an opaque projector, so you can use any photograph or drawing rather than a transparency.) Adjust the focus and placement of the projector until the picture fits the wall as desired. Use the image on the front of the paint-by-number package as a guide.

6. Make sure the projector is level and stable. Tape the legs to the floor, if needed.

7. Use a pencil to lightly trace the projected shapes and corresponding numbers onto the wall (see photo A). (We chose to use only the center portion of our picture and removed some details, including the deer, in our forest scene.)

8. Begin work on the wall, using a large artist brush to paint in the first color. Start with the larger areas and most recognizable shapes, such as tree trunks and branches. Fill in remaining areas with corresponding colors, following your color code list (see photo B). Stand back from the painting often and check to see that it resembles the image on the package front. (Some color differences may be very subtle. You can simplify the painting process by painting these areas the same color. If you do this too much, however, the painting may appear flat.)

9. After the painting is complete, add highlights where appropriate. For example, we added brighter highlights to the tops of the tree leaves to make the branches stand out. Let dry.

10. Create a softer, more unified surface by toning down the various hues with limewash that is lightly dry brushed over the entire surface. Dip just the tip of the brush into the limewash paint and tap it on a clean paper towel to remove excess. Quickly brush the limewash out in various directions, using random brush strokes until you have applied a thin, even coat. Repeat to cover entire mural surface. In areas where you have applied too much limewash, quickly blot away excess with a rag. Let dry.

SHOPPING LIST

- Paint-by-number kit
- Computer and scanner with Adobe Photoshop program (optional)
- Acrylic craft paint in various colors
- Latex paint for base coat
- 3" and 4" chip brushes
- Image projector and stand
- Large flat and round artist brushes
- Resealable plastic paint containers
- Textured limewash finish
- Rags

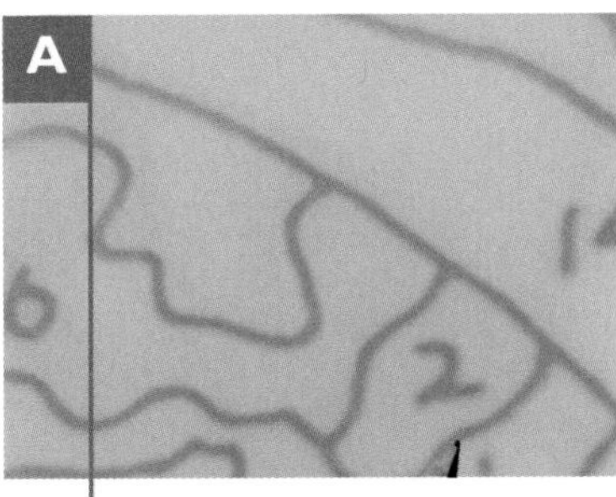

A

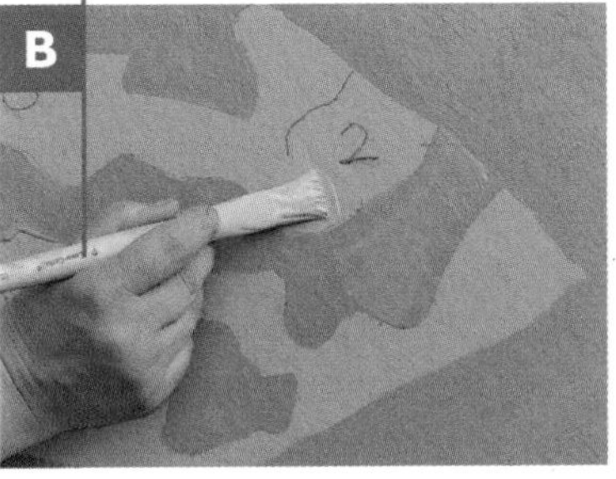

B

STENCILED *Jungle*

1. Base-coat the wall with white or a light cream color.

2. This mural is 5½ feet high by 7½ feet long, but stencil details can be added or subtracted so the mural will fit any size wall. Measure and mark the mural outline, then mask off with painters tape.

3. Prepare the forest background, including the tree line, mountains and sky. Starting at the bottom of the mural area, measure up 18 inches and 25 inches and make marks at both ends of the mural. Snap a chalk line across mural area at each set of marks to create guidelines for drawing the tree line.

4. With pencil, draw a wavy line across the mural between the guidelines to represent the rounded treetops. Paint the area above the tree line with pale blue latex and the treetops and the wall area below with green latex. Let dry for 24 hours.

5. Measure and mark points 29 inches and 34 inches from the bottom of the mural and snap chalk lines to create guidelines for the mountaintops.

6. Draw an irregular line between the guidelines, this time with sharper peaks and valleys. Apply painters tape below the irregular line, following the contours.

7. To paint clouds, create a wash by mixing one cup of white latex paint with ⅛ cup of water. Dip a sea sponge into the wash and blot on paper towels. Only a small amount of paint should remain on the sponge. (As the paper towels become saturated with paint, replace them.)

8. Apply the wash more heavily right above the taped horizon line so that it is nearly white and sets off the horizon like clouds against a mountaintop. Use less wash as you move up toward the top of the mural, allowing more and more blue to show through. Let dry.

9. Mix a few drops of dark brown latex paint with about ¼ cup of green latex paint to make it slightly darker. Use a clean sea sponge to lightly apply paint along the edge of the treetops and randomly throughout the tree area to simulate leaves. Let dry for 24 hours.

10. Following the manufacturer's instructions, add layers of stencils to create your own scene, beginning with a layer of palm leaves. Tape your stencils on the wall to help determine placement of mural elements. Stencil trees and vines first. Let dry. Add smaller leaves, grasses, animals and flowers and finish with a border stencil (see photo A).

SHOPPING LIST

- Flat latex paint in white, pale blue, green and dark brown (for background) and light and medium brown (for large trees)
- Yardstick level
- Painters tape
- Chalk line
- Container for glaze
- Paper towels
- Sea sponges
- Rainforest mural stencil kit
- Acrylic craft paint in various colors (for stencils)
- Stencil brushes

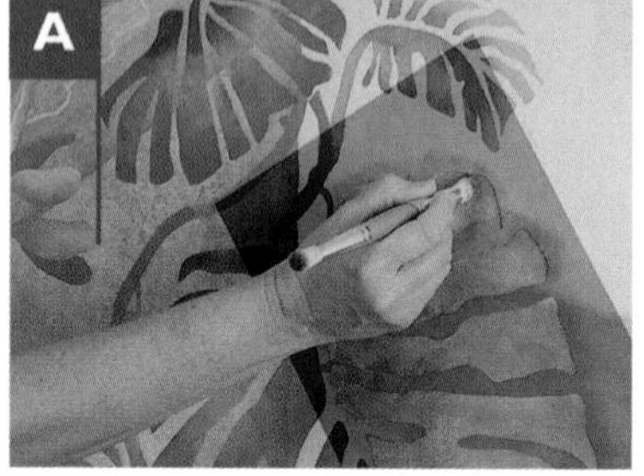

A

MANY COMPANIES SELL STENCIL KITS designed to help you create stunning effects and scenes. In most cases, you'll begin with basic stencils, such as bricks, rocks, trellises, hills, trees or window frames, using them to create a background. Next, add in other small elements, like birds and blooms. Embellish the scene with handpainted details—creating puffy clouds with a stippling brush or using an artist brush to add grass, veins on leaves or cracks in stone.

TIP: *If you paint with a partner, be aware that there will be differences in style. For continuity, one person should work on the background—the other should add the details.*

MAGNIFIED *Monet*

CREATING THE GRID

1. Base-coat the wall with dark teal. Let dry.

2. Select your artwork. You may need to use a portion of the original artwork rather than the entire piece in order to create an equal number of grid squares on the print and the wall. (For example, our wall was 8 feet by 8 feet. We chose a 16-inch by 16-inch portion of the 16½-inch by 23-inch print to highlight the water lilies. Our wall was divided into sixteen 2-foot squares and our print area was divided into sixteen 4-inch squares.) Divide the print and wall into an equal number of squares. More detailed images may require smaller grids to help you transfer the intricate designs.

3. Mark the grid on the print or a color photocopy of the print, using the lines of a quilters ruler (see photo A). Choose a pen or pencil color that will show up against the entire print.

4. Use a yardstick level and light chalk that shows up against the base coat to measure and mark the grid dimensions on the wall.

5. Using the gridded print as a guide, transfer the images and shapes from each print square to the corresponding wall square with chalk.

PAINTING THE MURAL

1. Look at squares on the print that you will be painting and choose colors that match. Dab the paint colors for the area on which you will be working onto a foam plate. Begin with the background. (We used several shades of blue, green and purple for the water. The water color varied in different areas of our print. Mix colors as needed.)

2. For the background, begin painting in one of the corner squares on the wall, referring to the same square on the print for a color guide. (Duplicate the feel of your print rather than the exact image. For our painting, we used loose, random brush strokes.) Start by painting the darkest shades first, add the lighter shades next and highlights last. Stand back occasionally to get a better perspective of the painting and add touches of dark or light colors as needed to create a balanced look. To help the paint flow better, dip the brush in water occasionally as you work. Let background dry.

3. Paint details last (see photo B), using the techniques as above. (We used teal, aqua, white and touches of cranberry for the lily pads and white and yellow for the water lilies.)

SHOPPING LIST

- Flat latex paint in dark teal
- Monet art print (we used Effects at the Evening)
- Marking pen
- Yardstick level
- Quilters ruler
- Chalk
- Foam plate or palette
- Artist paintbrushes (we used 1" flat brushes)
- Acrylic craft paint in white, opaque yellow, cranberry, aqua, navy, deep sky blue, teal, and denim blue

A

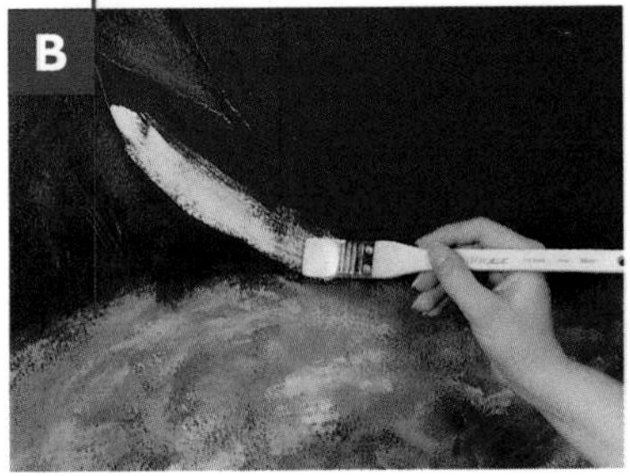
B

ON THE GRID

IF YOU'VE EVER COMPLETED A GRID drawing in a children's activity book, you've got the ability to create a mural. This simple technique involves marking a grid on an art print and marking the same number of grid squares on the wall. The image is transferred to the wall, one square at a time. The grid squares allow you to view each design element separately. Visible brush strokes and freeform style make a Claude Monet water lily painting a good choice for a novice painter. If you don't feel comfortable painting freehand, use transfer paper behind your enlarged pattern pieces and trace the design onto your wall.

OP Art

RECTANGLES AND OTHER QUADRILATERAL SHAPES in vivid colors create unique wall art with a contemporary flair. Plan the dimensions and placement of your mural, taking wall size and furniture placement into consideration. We placed our bottom line 46 inches from the floor and the top line 24 inches above that, with the mural running the length of the wall. Use a yardstick level to mark the horizontal guidelines on the wall with pencil. If your design won't span the wall, draw vertical lines to mark the ends. Place tape to the outside of the mural guidelines and paint the mural area cream. Let dry and remove tape, then apply ¼" painters tape across the wall following the inside of the guidelines. Base-coat the wall around the mural guidelines with orange paint. Measure and mark a horizontal guideline centered between the top and bottom guidelines. Apply ¼" tape over this guideline. Divide the space vertically with ¼" tape to create 12" square panels. (Adjust panel size to fit your mural.) Inside each panel, use ¼" and 1" painters tape to randomly mask off shapes. Create freeform four-sided designs in various sizes, nesting smaller shapes within larger ones. Paint each panel using foam brushes and bright green, purple, yellow, red and orange acrylic craft paints so you achieve a balanced color distribution. (Keep in mind that cream paint will be visible between inset shapes after you remove the tape.)

WELL-TRAVELED

CREATE AMBIENCE WITH A MURAL of an old-world map in muted colors. Select any map from around the world to create a personalized room. For example, try a map of Italy for the dining room or one of Scotland for a golfer's office. Base-coat the wall with a background color that will become the water. Using suede paint will give the wall the look and texture of old leather. Project the image onto the wall with an image projector. Enlarge the image to cover the wall, but be aware of your desired furniture placement. Focus the image as clearly as possible, making sure any lettering is straight. Trace all the lines of the map onto the wall with chalk. With a rag or sponge, colorwash a few layers of watered-down paint onto the land masses in a new color that will subtly contrast with the water and the room. The chalk will brush off easily when the paint dries and the suede base coat absorbs the paint to enhance its texture. Outline the newly colored land with a subtle color that fits in with the furniture. For an extra flourish, add details such as boats, text and a compass rose. For contrast, use acrylic craft paint colors that will stand out against the background.

BOLD Blooms

PAINT AND OVERSIZE FLOWER CUTOUTS team up to make a bold statement. For the background, mimic the blooms' watercolor feel with washes of yellow and green atop a creamy white base coat. After applying the base coat, mix gold and olive green glazes in separate containers using flat latex paint and glaze. Just before applying the glaze, wipe a large, water-soaked sponge across the entire mural area. This will allow the wash to flow smoothly during application. You may need to re-wet areas as you work. Beginning in one corner, use a chip brush to apply alternating yellow and green washes to the perimeter of the mural area. Work in 2-foot sections and blend in toward the center of the wall (see photo A). The color should appear darkest at the perimeter, fading to a pale yellow in the center. Complete the entire mural area, wiping heavy areas with a damp rag or wet brush and filling in light areas with additional washes. (Do not overwork; this may lift off the first layers of paint. If this occurs, let dry completely and reapply). While washes are still wet, drip water from a wet chip brush onto the wall in select areas for a streaked effect. Tape flower cutouts onto the wall at desired height and draw stems freehand with pencil. Also mark flower placement on wall with pencil. Determine where you will place shadows and highlights, referring to a light source in the room, such as a window, as your guide. With artist brushes, paint the stems using washes made from several shades of green acrylic paint, using the darkest color for shadows and thinned white paint to make highlights (see photo B). Try to paint tops of stems so they blend with the foliage color on the cutouts. When the stems are complete, place the cutouts, which are prepasted like wallpaper, facedown and wet the backs with a damp sponge. Position on wall at marked locations and press in place, smoothing out bubbles. If desired, seal the entire wall and mural with a water-based, non-yellowing polyacrylic satin sealer.

A

B

TOOL *Tricks*

IF YOU'RE LOOKING FOR A DISTINCTIVE WAY to add pattern and depth to your walls, you don't have to spend a mint on fancy paint applicators from specialty shops. Sometimes inspiration comes from the most unexpected of sources—like the broom closet, garage or garden shed. Just pair hardworking household helpers, like chamois cloth, rakes, brushes and brooms with paints and glazes to create effects that range from subtly textured to striking.

ACCESSORY

CHAMOIS *Style*

1. Base coat entire wall with silvery-gray paint. Let dry.

2. Twist chamois around the roller and pin into place at the ends of the roller using T pins (see photo A). Wrap one medium-sized chamois around the entire roller or cut it in two and wrap one around as above, wrapping the second one between the rolls of the first to add more texture. (If you choose to pin your chamois at the center, be sure the pin does not stick up or it may interfere with the treatment.)

3. Mix one part taupe paint with one part glaze and pour into paint pan. Apply a medium amount of paint to the roller. Starting at the bottom of the wall at the corner of the room, roll paint onto the wall (see photo B) and continue up to the ceiling to create a stripe. (As the roller goes up the wall, the paint becomes more translucent, so you may want to vary the pressure.)

4. Starting at the bottom again, apply paint in the same manner right next to the first stripe. In order to create balance, we started our application at the bottom for about eight rows then reversed it and started at the top for eight rows. We alternated the application in this manner all the way around the room to create a light and dark variation. (Wall dimensions will vary from home to home and the rows will probably not work out evenly around the room; make up the difference at the corners by adjusting the size of your roller and painting narrower or wider stripes there.)

5. Touch up any areas that have been rolled on too heavily by immediately patting the spot with a dry paper towel. Use a new towel every time or the paint will smudge. Do not roll over any area too many times or the image will become blurred. Let dry.

SHOPPING LIST

- Chamois (purchased at auto-supply store)
- Flat latex paint in silvery gray and taupe
- Glaze base
- 12" paint roller cover with cardboard center
- T pins
- Paper towels

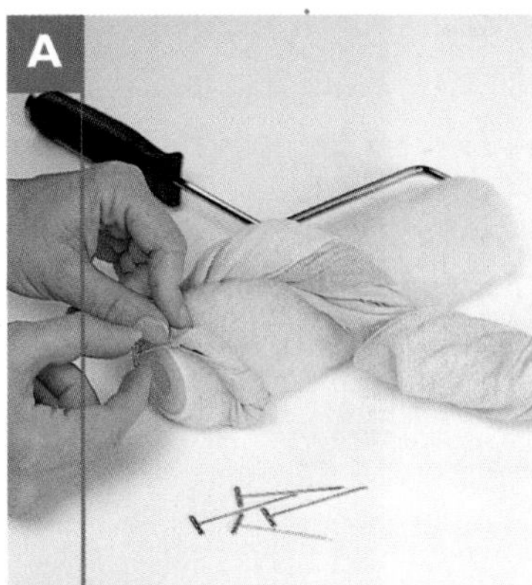
A

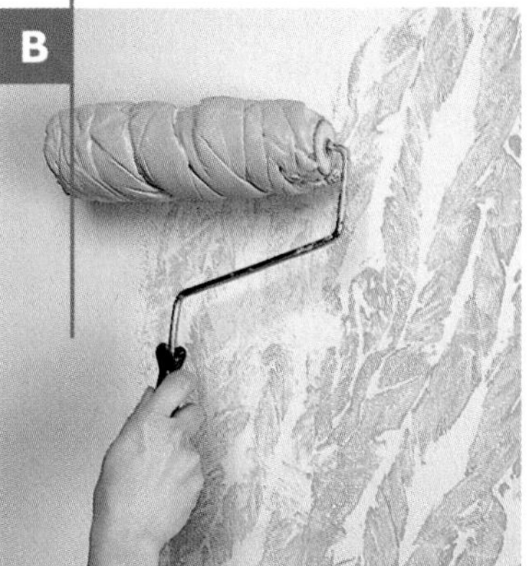
B

TEXTURED ROLLER COVERS

TO GET ANOTHER GREAT TEXTURED EFFECT with a paint roller cover, wrap it with bunched-up plastic wrap and staple to secure. This will produce a soft, mottled pattern similar to bagging. Or, look for a specialty roller or decorative roller cover at your local paint or home improvement center. You might find such styles as honeycomb, stippling, sponge, braid and more, available in a variety of sizes. Some manufacturers even make patterned roller covers meant for creating borders or allover designs that mimic stencils or wallpaper.

SWIRLS OF *Silver*

SHOPPING LIST

- Flat latex paint in aqua blue
- Yardstick level
- Colored pencil to match wall color
- Wide painters tape
- Heavy gel matte medium
- Acrylic craft paint in silver
- Mixing container with snap-on lid
- Spatula
- Small fine-bristled scrub brush
- Chip brush
- Shaper tool with chisel tip

1. Base-coat wall with aqua blue paint.

2. Use colored pencil and yardstick level to mark 6-inch horizontal stripes on the wall, alternating with 3-inch stripes in between.

3. Mask off each side of 6-inch stripes with painters tape.

4. Mix 10 parts of the heavy gel medium with one part silver acrylic in a container with a snap-on lid. Use a spatula or paint stick to mix thoroughly. (Keep the lid on the container when the paint is not in use.)

5. Trowel a thin layer of mixed gel on to about a 2-foot area of a stripe (see photo A).

6. Use a small scrub brush to create a circular pattern in the gel by rotating the scrub brush in one hand, pivoting around one end. Repeat the motion, overlapping shapes as desired until the gel-covered area of the stripe is filled with silver-colored disk shapes (see photo B). (Be careful not to spread medium onto the 3-inch stripes; if this happens, clean surface immediately.) Scrape excess medium from the sides of brush with a spatula and return it to the container. Continue working across the stripe, first troweling on medium, then texturizing with the scrub brush. Complete all the 6-inch stripes. Remove tape.

7. Use a chip brush to make a freehand horizontal band (about 1½ inches wide) down the center of a 3-inch stripe, working on an area about 18 inches long (see photo C). (The gel sets quickly, so do not overextend your work area.)

8. Use the color-shaper tool to scribe a wavy line down the center of the brush-stroked line, revealing the painted wall below. To create the thin-to-thick wavy line, hold the tool at the same angle as you glide across the band, moving up and down to create the waves. (Do not rotate the tool in your hand; it is designed to be used like a calligraphy pen.)

9. Continue creating the brush-stroked band along the length of the 3-inch stripe, blending the new area with the previous work, and repeat the process for scribing a wavy line as above. Hold the shaper tool at the correct angle to blend in the new stroke with the old. Repeat to complete the rest of the 3-inch stripes.

USING SHAPER TOOLS

THESE SILICONE-TIPPED PAINTING TOOLS come in a variety of shapes and sizes that allow you to move wet paint around and carve images into painted surfaces. Unlike bristles of a brush, they do not spread out, giving you more control in creating designs, similar to drawing with a pencil. A flat chisel creates stripes and flat, even strokes. Use a cup round to achieve soft edges or make dots. Or, choose an angle chisel for freeform strokes and thick-to-thin lines similar to those seen in calligraphy.

A

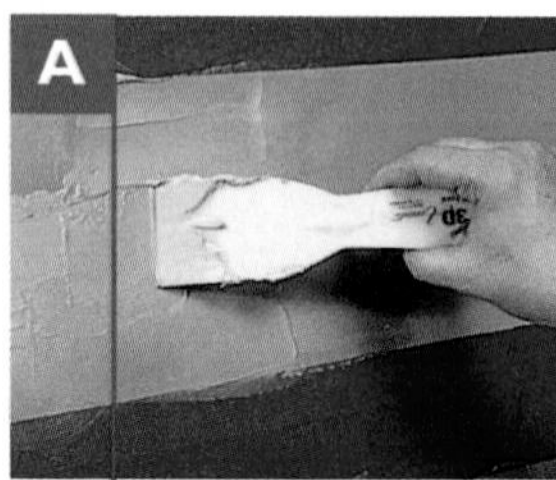

B

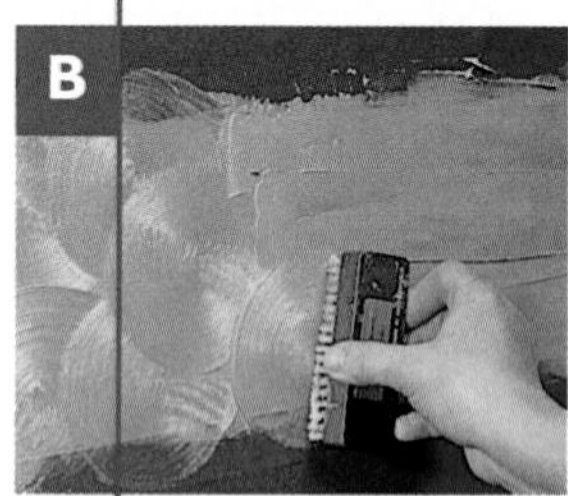

C

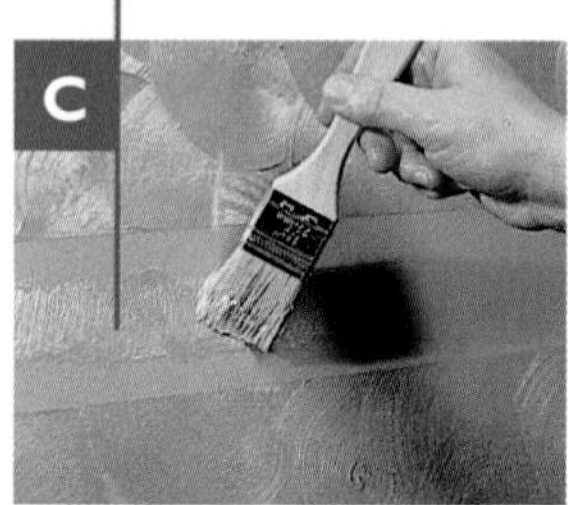

STRONG *Impressions*

1. Base-coat walls with white latex paint. Let dry.

2. Use needle-nose pliers to create various swirl shapes out of armature wire. We created our wire shapes with a little extra wire on the end to use for a handle. The swirl shape must be flat in order for it to be imprinted completely when pressed into the stone medium. Also cut 3-inch squares of wire mesh.

3. Apply a liberal amount of stone medium to a 4-foot by 4-foot section of the wall. Use the Japan scraper to drag the medium across the wall, creating imperfections in the application and making sure that the treatment is not entirely smooth. The more texture, the more interesting the finished result. (You may wish to work with a partner, one person spreading the medium and the other imprinting objects.) As a team, you can work in a slightly larger area.

OTHER IMPRINTS

THIS TECHNIQUE USES SMALL OBJECTS pressed into a stone medium to build texture. We used swirl-shaped armature wire, wire mesh and drywall anchors. You could also use old keys, paper clips, buttons or any other small object with an interesting shape. Thin, wirelike items are best for working with the wet medium. Before working on the walls, apply a layer of stone medium to a practice board and imprint various objects into the medium to determine whether the designs will be appealing.

4. Press one item at a time into the wet stone medium, then slowly remove it. For the spiral, use even pressure and press into wall using the wire handle, evening out the spiral with your fingers if needed (see photo A).

5. Roll drywall anchors across surface to create tracklike marks (see photo B). Press or roll pieces of wire mesh onto surface using heavier or lighter pressure for an interesting effect (see photo C). If you are not satisfied with any impression, immediately smooth it over with the scraper and try again. Continue imprinting the objects into the wall in a balanced, but random, fashion until you achieve the desired effect. Let dry.

6. Mix one part spring green paint with three to four parts glaze.

7. Apply the glaze mixture to a 1-foot by 1-foot section of the wall with a paintbrush, making sure paint gets into all of the grooves and crevices. Blend out at the edges of the section.

8. Wipe away excess glaze with a rag (see photo D). Change rags as they become saturated. Continue rubbing the glaze mixture into the wall. Rub lightly around the imprints and more vigorously around the flat surfaces to create color variation in the treatment and highlight the designs.

9. Continue applying glaze as above until the entire wall has been covered.

SHOPPING LIST

- Flat latex paint in white and spring green
- Armature wire
- 2" paintbrush
- Needle-nose pliers
- Wire mesh
- Textured paint
- Drywall anchors or other small objects
- Glaze base
- Stainless-steel Japan scraper
- Rags or paper towels

A

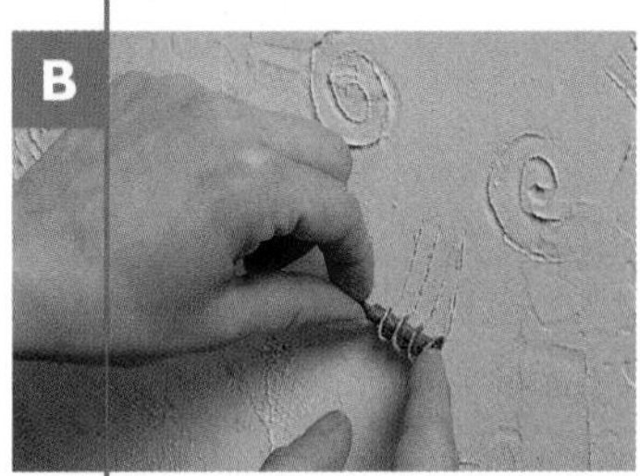

B

C

D

SWEPT *Away*

POUNCE WHITE PAINT AND GLAZE over a honey-colored base coat using a kid's broom for a softly textured wall. Base-coat wall with honey-gold paint. Let dry. In a paint tray, mix one part white paint with five parts glaze. Fill another paint tray with white paint. Dip just the tips of a child-size broom into the white paint. Use some newspaper or an old towel to remove excess paint from the broom; too much paint will leave drops and blobs on the wall. Start at the top of the wall and work across and down. Begin to pounce the white paint on the wall with the broom (see photo), making sure to turn the broom as you work to get different effects. Work in irregular sections; it is best to have an uneven look. Dip the tips of the broom in the glaze mixture and apply to the next section as above. Wait a minute after completing a section, then go back and softly swirl the paint together in some areas, still using the broom. The edges should blend, and the gold base coat should not be completely covered. This gives the walls a powdery look. While painting, step back and look at the treatment to determine where additional paint is needed. Repeat, alternating straight paint and glaze mixture, until walls are complete.

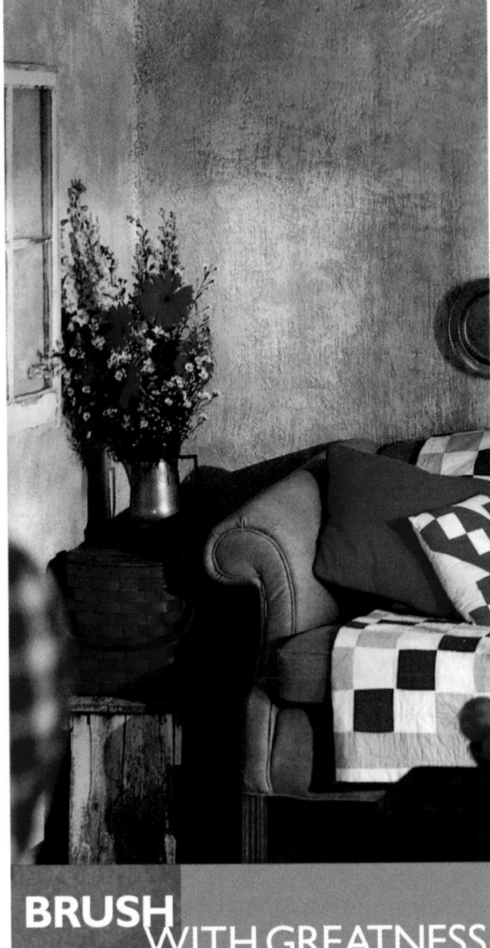

BRUSH WITH GREATNESS

TEAM RAG ROLLING AND A WALLPAPER BRUSH for a textured wall with the look of faded denim. Start with a base coat of white satin-finish paint. Let wall dry overnight. In separate containers, mix light blue and medium blue paints with paint conditioner, using one part conditioner to two parts paint. Dip a crumpled shop towel into the medium blue mixture and randomly dab the paint on the wall in a 2-foot by 2-foot section. Take a clean crumpled shop towel in your other hand and use it to dab off excess paint. Complete the walls in this manner. Apply the light blue paint mixture using the same technique, but allowing some of the medium blue to show through in spots. Dip a dry wallpaper brush in medium blue-gray paint and remove excess by tapping the brush against the edge of the paint tray. Swiftly drag the brush down the painted walls to create depth (see photo).

RAKISH *Flair*

A PLASTIC SHRUB-AND-EVERGREEN RAKE is key to creating this cross-hatched pattern. This treatment requires a two-person team for best results because glaze dries so quickly. One person should apply the glaze mixture and the second can do the raking technique (see photo). Base-coat your wall with flat white paint and let dry. Mix five parts glaze with one part cocoa paint. Remove the rake handle for ease in applying even pressure to the wall. Plan to complete one entire wall at a time, starting at the ceiling in one corner and working down to the baseboard as you move across the wall. Apply glaze with a ⅜"-nap roller without stopping to avoid overlapping glaze strokes. Immediately follow the glaze application with the rake, holding it at a 70- to 90-degree angle to the wall and pulling it through the glaze using a small sweeping motion. Vary the direction of the rake to create an interesting pattern. Overlap areas so no area is left untouched. Continue the raking technique across the wall from the ceiling to the floor. As you work, clean the rake tines often with paper towels; they will become coated with glaze.

AT THE CAR WASH

POLISH SOME CHROME OR ADD POLISH TO YOUR WALLS—the same tool can serve both purposes. For a treatment similar to sponging, but with a softer, more blended effect, try a chenille-pile car-wash pad. Select two similar hues. (We used light and medium ocean blue.) Base-coat wall with the lighter color and let dry. Mix the darker color with glaze base, using one part of each. Dampen the car-wash pad slightly with water and dip into the paint-glaze mixture. Dab the pad onto the wall randomly, turning it frequently to build a flecked effect.

MOVEABLE *Walls*

120

122

124

125

IT'S A GOOD BET that many rooms in your house serve more than one purpose. Whether you've got an eat-in kitchen or a home office tucked into a corner of your bedroom, you might find yourself using a space in more ways than one. If you've ever felt you needed an extra wall, here's a way to get one without hiring a carpenter. These easy-to-assemble room dividers are a great, nonpermanent way to reshape your space and add a unique design element as well.

RESIST TECHNIQUES

TO GET A CHIPPY, peeling paint surface without the passage of years, faux painters use various products to act as a barrier between multiple paint layers. In places where the resistant material is applied, the topcoat scrapes away easily. Here, rubber cement acts as a resist between the two layers of paint, allowing you to remove the top layer of white paint to reveal the aqua underneath. Other compounds used in a similar fashion are petroleum jelly, paste wax and candle wax. Each produces a slightly different effect.

ROLLING *Wall*

1. Remove alternating panels from the doors and replace them with chicken wire. Start by drilling a ⅜" hole in each corner of the panel (see photo A). The holes should be large enough to accommodate the jigsaw blade.

2. Saw from one hole to the other to remove the panel (see photo B). Remove any leftover pieces from the channels in the door frame. Fill the grooves with spackle, let dry, then sand.

3. Base-coat the doors with aqua paint.

4. With wire cutters, cut pieces of chicken wire ½ inch larger all around than the panel opening. For a more substantial look, use two layers of chicken wire to cover each opening.

5. Staple the wire to the back of the door to cover the opening. Before stapling, you may need to add dollhouse trim or other thin, flat wood shims to level the top and bottom of the opening.

6. With a miter box and backsaw, cut pieces of ¾" screen molding to frame the wire panels and cover the wire on the front and back of the doors. Tap brads through molding, then set into place on door. Sink brad heads with a nail set (see photo C).

7. Smear thick layers of rubber cement randomly over panels where desired, including places where paint naturally wears, such as edges. Let the rubber cement dry to the touch.

8. Let the paint dry to the touch, then use a chisel to lightly scrape over the surface to lift paint off in areas where you applied rubber cement. Rub the area with your fingers or sandpaper to loosen and remove the remaining rubber cement and paint. Do not let the topcoat sit too long or apply too much paint; it may be more difficult to remove.

9. Place the two sets of folded doors on top of each other. Attach three evenly spaced hinges to the middle edges where the sets meet.

10. To make the screen movable, add wheels to the base of the doors. Drill a ⅜" hole into the bottom end of the wood door frame and tap the socket in place with a hammer. Push the stem of the wheel into the socket to lock in place. Use at least one wheel per corner to support the screen as it folds up.

11. To provide ample support, mount the screen to a wall. Cut a 1 x 4 to the length of the screen, minus the width of your baseboard molding. Mount the 1 x 4 vertically on the wall just above the baseboard, aligning the top edge with the top of the screen. Attach hinges to 1 x 4 so the barrel of each hinge is flush with the front edge of the board. Attach the other half of each hinge to the edge of the folded screen.

SHOPPING LIST

- Two 30" bifold doors (ours were 78 inches tall with each door measuring 15 inches wide)
- Chicken wire
- Staple gun with ¼" staples
- Wire cutters
- Flat latex paint in aqua and white
- 1½" plastic wheel casters
- Drill and ⅜" drill bit
- Three sets of 2" x 3" hinges
- 7" length of 1 x 4 board
- Dollhouse trim or craft wood (for use as shims)
- ¾"-wide screen molding
- Jigsaw
- Miter box and backsaw
- Chisel
- Brad nails
- 100-grit sandpaper
- Spackling compound

A

B

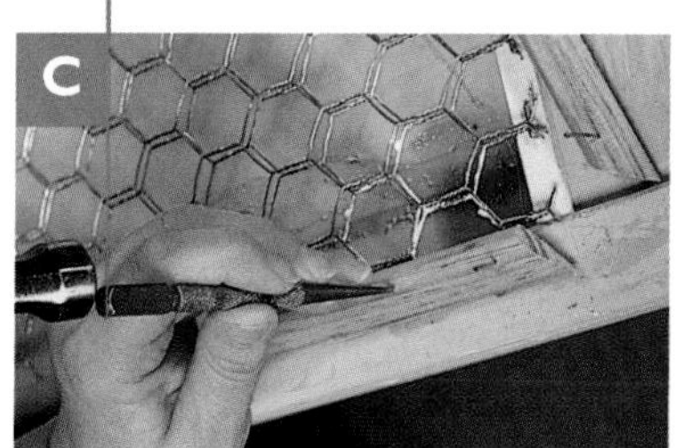
C

BITS AND *Pieces*

1. Remove the hinges from both sets of doors. Separate the doors and set aside as pairs.

2. For the tall center pair of doors, use a jigsaw to cut off the smallest panel, above the rail, from each door. (Our doors each had three paneled areas—a small one on top and two larger ones below.) Sand edges with 100-grit sandpaper. For the smaller side doors, use a jigsaw to remove the lower large panels, cutting below the rail.

3. Base-coat doors pink. Let dry. Set the shorter pair of doors aside.

4. Lay center doors flat. Center mirrors on top panels and trace with pencil. Use a carpenters square to ensure mirrors are aligned.

5. Using a drill and a spade bit, cut a hole ⅛" to ¼" inside the pencil line. Insert jigsaw blade in hole. Cut out mirror shapes just inside of the pencil line (see photo A). This allows mirrors to rest against openings. Sand cut edges and set mirrors aside.

6. Using painters tape, mask off evenly spaced stripes, about 1 inch apart, on the top paneled areas of both center doors. Dry brush exposed stripes with spruce green. Let dry. Dry brush green stripes with white craft paint. Remove tape. Let dry.

7. Arrange all four doors on flat surface. Rotate shorter side doors so the small paneled areas are at the bottom.

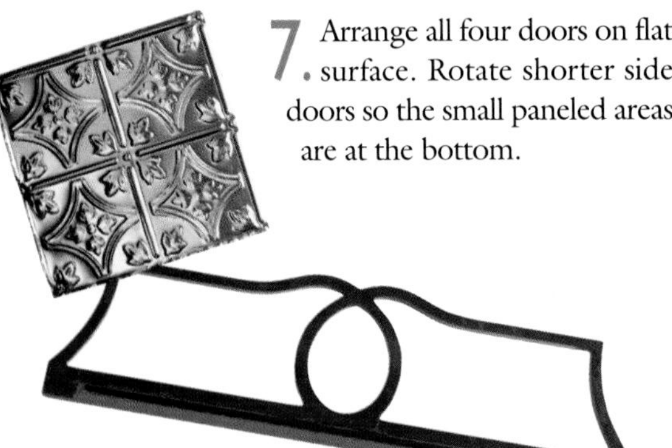

8. Plan placement of wallpaper, decorative tin sheeting or painted wood appliqués on remaining door panels for a balanced overall design.

9. Cut pieces of wallpaper to fit inside selected panels. For prepasted paper, wet and smooth onto panel using a damp sponge (see photo B). If it is not prepasted, apply wallpaper adhesive, following manufacturer's instructions. For a finished look, hot glue white braided trim around the edges.

10. Paint various wood appliqués with spruce green, pink and cherry red. Let dry. Arrange appliqués in selected panels and adhere with construction adhesive (see photo C). Let dry. Dry brush entire paneled area with lavender. Let dry. Dry brush with white craft paint. Let dry.

11. Use tin snips to cut decorative tin to fit inside selected panels. Paint tin with lavender. Let dry. Dry brush with white craft paint. Let dry. Attach tin to door with upholstery tacks (see photo D).

12. Place center doors facedown and side by side on a flat surface. Join doors with two mending plates, placed on the back, one 6 inches from the top and one 6 inches from the bottom.

13. Because the side doors have been shortened and flipped over, original hinge holes will not align. Drill new holes and attach side doors to center doors with original hardware.

14. On the back of each door, apply mirror mastic adhesive around the edge of the oval cutout and secure the mirrors in place. Let dry. Hot glue red cording around the outside of the oval cutouts to frame the mirrors.

SHOPPING LIST

- Two sets of bifold doors
- Drill with driver bit and ½" spade bit
- Jigsaw
- 100-grit sandpaper
- Flat latex paint in pink, lavender, spruce green and cherry red
- Paintbrushes
- Two mirrors
- Pencil
- Carpenters square
- 1" painters tape
- Floral wallpaper
- Scissors
- Damp sponge or wallpaper adhesive
- Glue gun and glue
- White braided trim
- Architectural accents, like wood appliqués, decorative brackets, finials, etc.
- Clear construction adhesive
- Decorative tin sheeting
- Tin snips
- Upholstery tacks
- Hammer
- 2" mending plates
- Mirror mastic adhesive
- 2 yards of red cording

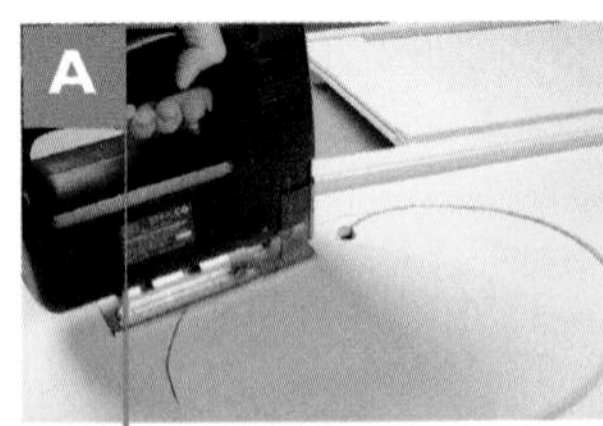
A

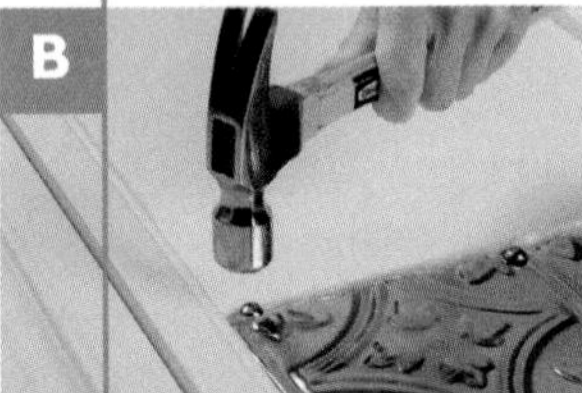
B

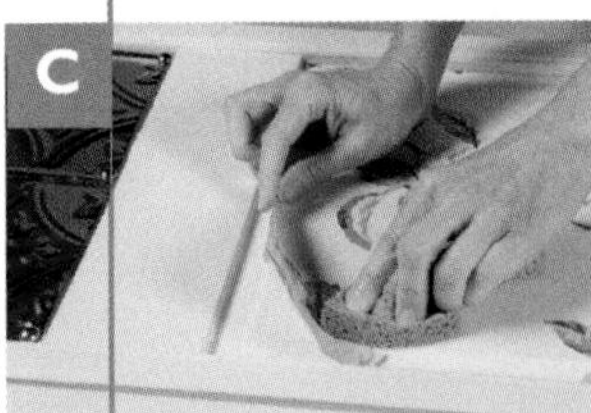
C

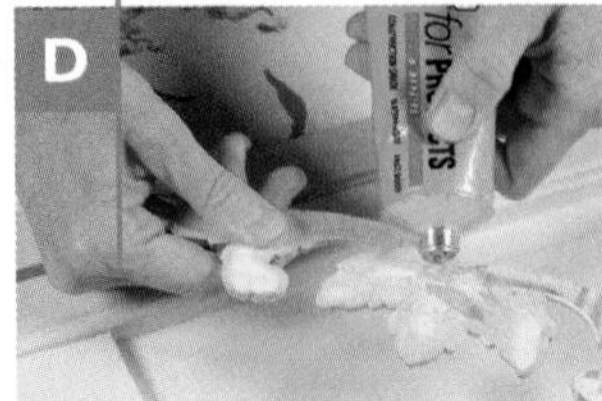
D

SHOWSTOPPING TOPPER

AS A FINISHING TOUCH, decorate the top of each screen panel using architectural elements, flea-market finds, trim or finials. We created a topper to span the center doors from a piano music rack and used finials with a wood appliqué on one side door and a spindle bracket on the other. Paint the pieces to coordinate. Attach using adhesive, mending plates and screws.

DRESSED-UP *Divider*

THIS FOLDING SCREEN RECALLS CHILDHOOD paper dolls, with its couture cutouts snipped from scrapbook papers. Start with a three-panel unfinished wood changing screen (available at major craft stores). Sand the screen and wipe with a cloth, then paint it celery green (or another color to match your wallpaper). Using a craft knife and straight edge, measure and cut pieces of foamboard to fit the screen panel openings, with a ¾-inch overlap on all sides for attaching to the screen. Cut two pieces of foam-core for each opening. Using a quilters ruler, measure and mark pieces of wallpaper to fit each foam-core piece, allowing 2 inches extra all around to wrap over the edges (see photo). Plan each wallpaper piece at the same pattern repeat so the panels will look uniform. Cut out wallpaper pieces and use spray mount to attach them to the foam-core pieces. Smooth out any bubbles with a burnishing tool, like a plastic pan scraper. Fold the four edges to the back, mitering the corners and trimming, if needed. Secure in place with decoupage medium. Create several freehand dress patterns in desired sizes and determine scrapbook paper choices for each one. Use transfer paper and a pencil to copy the patterns onto the scrapbook paper. Use a paint marker in a coordinating color (we used crimson to go with our pink papers) to trace the dress outlines. Cut out dresses, leaving a narrow border around the marker outlines. Lay out dress cutouts on the panels to determine placement. We used three evenly spaced dresses per panel, tipping each dress in a different direction for interest. Apply decoupage medium to the back of each dress to secure to the panels. Working on one side of the screen, center panels over the openings, with a ¾-inch overlap on all sides, and secure in place with white tacky glue. Clamp and lay flat to dry overnight. Repeat to attach remainder of panels on the other side of the screen. For added support, tap small nails into the corners of each panel and cover nail heads with upholstery tacks.

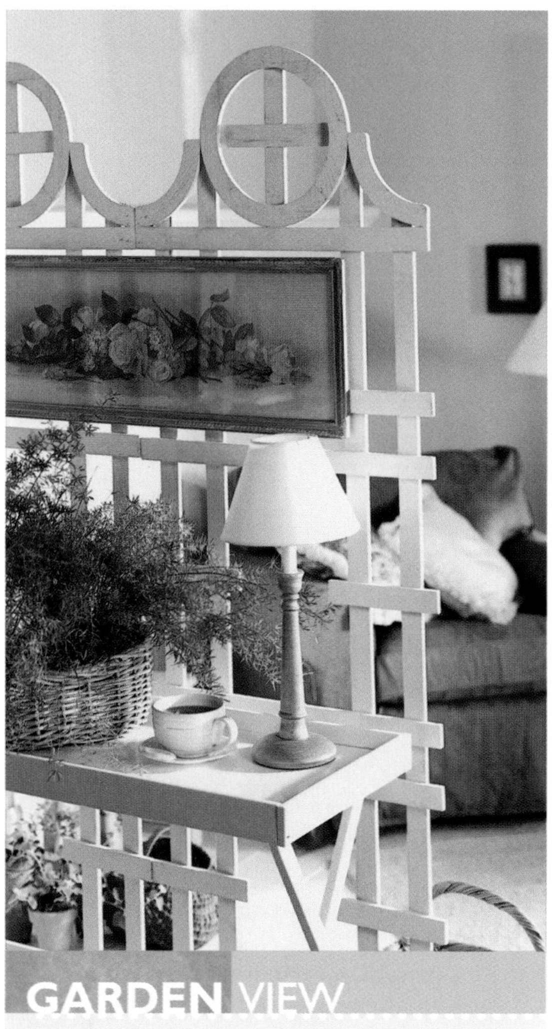

GARDEN VIEW

IF YOU DON'T HAVE AN ENTRYWAY, a simple divider made from a pair of garden trellises and a sofa table can create a separate space for welcoming guests into your home. Paint two redwood trellises white, then join them side by side with mending plates. You can also use an arbor or section of lattice for a similar effect. We found a tray-style sofa table whose crisscrossed legs echo the simple, straight lines of the trellises. Use any style of table, cupboard or chest, but make sure that whatever furniture piece you select looks good from the back as well as the front. A framed print of garden roses further enhances the wall effect by unifying the trellises. To make sure the unit is stable, attach the trellis to the back edge of the table with L brackets. For stability, secure one side of the trellis unit to a wall with several metal L brackets placed at the top, middle and bottom. Paint them to match the wall later. Attach the trellis unit to the floor in a few spots in the same manner.

TUB *Surround*

AN OLD PAINTED SCREEN DOOR adds privacy as a divider between a sink and bathtub. Adding a shelf and coat hooks to the sink side of the door provides storage for bath essentials and a place to hang a bathrobe and towels. We hung out door as we found it. If you are using a door that has loose or chipping paint, apply sealer. For the shelf, cut a 1 x 4 to fit the door width and attach it with 1¾" screws from the back side. Paint new pieces added for structure to match the door. Attach three coat hooks, two on one side and one on the other side. Under the shelf, attach three 1" mug hooks. Attach the door to the wall using three 3" hinges spaced evenly along the side. Secure the door to the floor with two 2" L brackets. For added stability, attach two lengths of 1 x 2 to extend to the ceiling from the top of the door on each side. Cover the joined area with two decorative cabinet-knob backing plates and screws. Fasten 1 x 2s to the ceiling with L brackets on the back of the door. Paint the backing plates and L brackets to match the door. If desired, use a decorative sign or glass window piece to fill in the space between the door and the ceiling.

Index

Sources

Pages 8, 27, 42, 101
Textured limewash finish: Special Effects Textured Limewash, McCloskey Special Effects; call 800-767-2532 or visit www.valspar.com.

Pages 9, 82, 112-113
Shaper tools: Colour Shaper tools, Royal Sovereign; www.colourshaper.com; available through Dick Blick Art Materials; call 800-828-4548 or visit www.dickblick.com.

Page 42
Stone medium: LusterStone in Silver Moss, Faux Effects International; call 800-270-8871 or visit www.fauxfx.com.

Page 48
Stripe templates: Quick & Easy Stripes, Capé Designs; call 847-516-0400 or visit www.capedesigns.org.

Page 66
Gold leafing: Metalworks leafing adhesive kit and Kaleidoscope metal leafing flakes, Lefranc & Bourgeois; available at art and craft stores; call 800-445-4278 or visit www.lefranc-bourgeois.com.

Page 72
Floral spray paint: Design Master Color Tool, Design Master; call 800-525-2644 or visit www.dmcolor.com.

Page 76
Curtain wire and wall fittings: IKEA; call 800-434-IKEA or visit www.ikea.com.

Pages 100-101
Paint-by-number kit: Autumn Gold (CCPNS1), Reeves Paint by Number Classic Collection; available at major art and craft centers.

Pages 102-103
Stencil mural kit: Rainforest Mural (RF700AS), Stencil Ease; call 800-334-1776 or visit www.stencilease.com.

Credits

PROJECT DESIGNERS:

Dagmar Beasley, Christy Crafton, Jamie Dean, Debbie Egizio, Stephanie Fania, Barb Hookham, Melissa Howes-Vitek, Kathy Huddleston, Marge Jackson, Maureen Looney, Leslie Ann Powers for Stencil Ease, Robin Reed, Michelle Rosales, Erin Vokoun

Find Great
Do-It-Yourself
Projects All Year Long
Subscribe to *Country Sampler Decorating Ideas*
Direct from the editors of *Walls That Wow!*, *Country Sampler Decorating Ideas* will help you create the home of your dreams. With each issue featuring up-to-the-minute home fashions, hot color combinations, new products, free patterns and step-by-step photography, it's the magazine designed to make you a success.
In Every Issue
• Picture-perfect paint projects
• Step-by-step instructions
• Decorating techniques
• Budget-friendly makeovers
• Space-stretching strategies
• Trash-to-treasure revivals
• Can-do designs for real people
To subscribe, call 800-678-9717 or visit our Web site at www.sampler.com today!